EVERY

po day is a em

sounds true
BOULDER, COLORADO

EVERY

po em

day is a

JACQUELINE SUSKIN

Find clarity, feel relief,
and see beauty in every moment

Sounds True
Boulder, CO 80306

Published 2020

Cover design by Rachael Murray
Book design by Meredith March

Printed in South Korea

Library of Congress Cataloging-in-Publication Data

Names: Suskin, Jacqueline, author.
Title: Every day is a poem : find clarity, feel relief, and see beauty
   in every moment / Jacqueline Suskin.
Description: Boulder : Sounds True, 2020.
Identifiers: LCCN 2019056625 (print) | LCCN 2019056626 (ebook) |
   ISBN 9781683644842 (paperback) | ISBN 9781683644859 (ebook)
Subjects: LCSH: Authorship—Psychological aspects. |
   Authorship—Problems, exercises, etc.
Classification: LCC PN171.P83 S87 2020 (print) | LCC PN171.P83
   (ebook) | DDC 808.02—dc23
LC record available at https://lccn.loc.gov/2019056625
LC ebook record available at https://lccn.loc.gov/2019056626

10 9 8 7 6 5 4 3 2 1

for Marlee Grace,
my soul mate in the work of poetic healing

When it's over, I want to say: all my life
I was a bride married to amazement.

—MARY OLIVER

contents

introduction

I am doing something I learned early to do, I am paying attention to small beauties.

—SHARON OLDS

*H*ow do humans deal with the heaviness of everyday living? How do we keep going when everything is so hard, sad, and infuriating? We're surrounded by hate, injustice, death, and destruction—how do we sift through the anguish and enjoy being alive?

My answer is, Poetry.

What would it be like to find inspiration everywhere you look? It's a sacred challenge to mine the wonder out of every day, out of trauma and pain, out of the mundane. This is what poetry does for us. No, it isn't a magic wand that vanishes all atrocity. But it does make humanity reappear; it brings beauty out of the shadow, back to the surface, making it accessible. Poetry is a guide, a teacher, providing reminders on how incredible it is to be alive at all, even when it hurts.

The poetic mind is a grateful one; it's a mind that celebrates the miracle of being. The poetic mind is moody, and it digs its heels into these moods, pulling out the best and worst of feelings in the name of discovery, in the name of the shared human condition. The poetic mind shines a light on its uniqueness and its specialized way of coping with grief or anger.

The strength of this mind is that it can turn any experience into one of worth, into something meaningful, into an answer or a gift of clarity.

When Allen Ginsberg wrote *Howl*, he tuned into the travesty of America in 1955, exposing the nuance of mental illness, connecting the dots between this sickness and the state of the country:

> I saw the best minds of my generation destroyed
> by madness, starving hysterical naked,
> dragging themselves through the negro streets at
> dawn looking for an angry fix . . .

This poem became an anthem as it brought out a new language to describe something so dark, painful, and prevalent. That's why *Howl* still sticks with us. Like all influential artworks, it displays a mind in touch with the greater picture, a mind that is willing to overflow with gratitude and wonder, while at the same time remaining skeptical and critical of society, war, and greed.

Similar in reach, Mary Oliver's famous poem "Wild Geese" remains impactful as it explores a universal permission to move through pain into awe by way of curiosity, acceptance, and a celebration of the intricate details that connect us all. Her words help us circle back to our innate imaginative power, a human quality that is available, all-inclusive, and reliably healing:

Whoever you are, no matter how lonely,
the world offers itself to your imagination.

    This is my purpose as a poet, to write reminders that help us identify with our place in the universe, on this perfect planet that we call home.

    I've always been a poet, filling notebooks with cryptic verse before I really even knew how to write properly. It's the way that my brain processes my experience. I even got a degree in poetry. From 2009–2019, my project Poem Store was my only job, and it enabled me to write more than forty thousand poems for strangers. I set up with my typewriter at private and public events, writing for patrons who chose a subject and a price in exchange for a unique poem that I wrote on the spot.

    This practice allowed me to explore the human condition in a way that I never dreamed possible. I've heard humanity's deepest secrets and traumas, I've listened to the most wonderful expressions of love and elation, I've witnessed intense confusion and beautiful awe—only to translate it all into poetry. When my customers saw themselves on the page, something happened. My words offered a reflection, a moment of deep knowing, and I provided written proof that they weren't alone, that they were seen and heard. This work is transformative and healing for people, and that's how I've been able to make my living as a poet in the modern day. My work fills a place in people's hearts, where there is a longing to be understood.

No matter where I am, no matter the demographic, no matter what part of the planet, everyone always asks me to write about the same subjects. They're all grieving over the same types of loss, celebrating the same kinds of pleasure, and longing for the same versions of love, devotion, and direction. My purpose is to decipher their feelings and reinforce their depths with poetry.

But outside of Poem Store, I still keep a dedicated daily writing practice. I continue to fill journals with rambling thoughts. I make myself turn the light on in the middle of the night if I have an idea to scribble down in a bedside notebook. I'm constantly working on a project and have six published books. My poetic mind never stops, and I notice how it bleeds into my nonwriting life as well.

I can walk down the street and appreciate the greatness of the world even if I've had a hard and emotional day. When it's difficult to be alive, I immediately look for the meaning that is intertwined in the hardship, and thus, the problem becomes my teacher. And when I feel an empathetic overload listening to the news on the radio, I find myself looking for the larger picture, the things that help me believe change is possible, that humanity has a chance, that hope is a bright light we all carry, and that I can tend to it with my craft as a poet.

I continuously turn to poetry for help. Mary Oliver's writing saves me when I feel too far from the forest. Wendell Berry's work rescues me when I feel disconnected from my intentions as an artist. Poets provide a new set of eyes that bring spark and magic into even the worst tragedy or most sluggish of slumps, marveling at the whole of creation and its wildness. Now more than ever, in a political climate where everyone's input is crucial, poetry can help us respond and express a call to action in beautiful and potent ways.

The poetic mind is the root of change. We'll always look to poets for the beginnings of true transformation. Poets are the caretakers of the human condition, the brave ones who speak out to instigate solutions to the larger problems of the heart and intellect. Everyone's voice matters, and when the society we live in shakes us into fear and heartache, the answer is to tune our collective poetic mind and call forth the newness we need. Poetry is not a dusty book on the shelf or a forgotten pastime of passion long dead. No, it's alive and well, at the forefront of resistance, and it thrives in the heart of activists everywhere.

You can be a casual poet, jotting down moments of inspiration, putting words to your most tender feelings, using pen and paper as an outlet for your rage, joy, and amusement. You may not realize it, but you're doing this already. This is the way we communicate now—we text, we comment, all in a condensed language that gets to the point quickly, that synthesizes heavy ideas in an efficient way, giving us quick doses of linguistic lessons that are accessible and easy to digest. Poetry helps us with focus and awareness; it inspires us to see beyond outward appearance, to find truths that are waiting to be revealed.

In this book, I'll show you some of my favorite aspects of poetry, from writing practices to pathways of expression and inspiration, alongside reminders that we all have the ability to create a mindset that weaves grandeur and import out of an otherwise difficult and often overwhelming existence. I'll suggest ways to use poetry as a tool for finding clarity and for feeling relief. This work offers up a habit of looking closer. It helps ignite curiosity about the smallest details, and it guides you to make a written document of splendor.

You can begin anywhere by following my directions from start to finish, or by flipping through and trying out some exercises and prompts. Maybe you'll enjoy the section on mapping your past and mining your memories, or perhaps you'll prefer to begin by indulging your senses. See how it feels to focus on awe in any moment. From the process of grieving the loss of a loved one, to the healing of a broken heart, poetry is a tool we can use to understand and appreciate all aspects of life.

Wherever this book leads you, its main goal is to settle you into a place of reverence, shifting your perspective so that you can use words to explore the wonder of being alive.

These are very uncertain times. Poetry won't cause brutality to vanish. But it might act as a healing tool, a soothing aid, or a transformative outlet.

Accept my invitation, and find that you have permission to be a poet in every moment. You have a relevant voice that we all need to hear, and your mentality can rest in a poetic place that will only enrich you, one gorgeous thought at a time.

chapter 1

BE IN AWE of EVERYTHING

And awe suddenly
passing beyond itself. Becomes
a form of comfort.

—DENISE LEVERTOV

When I zoom out on my life, I'm in awe of everything. It isn't just the tiny details that wow me; it's the way that they somehow fit into the giant fold of the universe. This fitting together, this wonder of small and large, this is the heart of poetry, and you can exercise it anywhere, anytime.

I fell in love with the word *awe* about eight years ago. I'm not sure how it came to me, but suddenly I found myself with three letters strung together that perfectly describe my most familiar state of being.

The common dictionary definition of awe is "a feeling of reverential respect mixed with fear or wonder." It's that "reverential respect" that I'm so often filled with when I take in our world. I like that fear is in there as well, not because I walk around afraid of the majesty that is life, but because it hints at the presence of death woven into the fabric of our impermanent existence. Our wonder is attached to the fleeting nature of our reality.

The fact that it could all be gone at any moment, that all of our experience is tangled up with so much pain and loss, is part of why it's so amazing to rejoice in every offering that life throws our way.

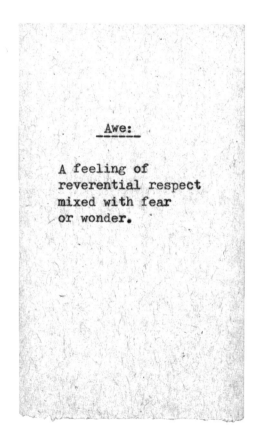

Awe:

A feeling of
reverential respect
mixed with fear
or wonder.

AWE IS THE CENTERPIECE OF ACCEPTANCE.

If we allow ourselves to practice awe in any situation, conjuring up a deep reverence for all things, we never miss the splendor or the importance of the moment. Awe is what allows me to meet life with my eyes open wide. It's my ever-growing admiration for the complexity of human understanding, and it's often my source of joy or pleasure in otherwise seemingly monotonous or trying times. Awe can also act as a verb. I can be awed by something. Awe is an active thing, it's coming at me from all angles, and it helps me accept the ephemeral nature of being human. Awe is an opportunity, and if you acquaint yourself with it, it becomes infinitely abundant and accessible.

Wherever you stand at any moment, whatever the situation, you can drum up a large dose of awe to get you through. Awe is appreciation. Awe is curiosity. It gets you to look closer, to lead with patience and compassion, awareness and intrigue. There is no shortage of fascination in the human spirit. We were born to ask why. We are here to make up our own answers. This is the poetry of being alive.

How can we be in awe of things that are horrific? Awe is not married to the light. We can be in awe of darkness. That feeling of breath leaving the body as you gasp in horror while watching the news, that's awe. All things hard or soft are amazing. This amazement comes from our ability to keep asking how and why. What's this all for? Where did it begin? Our stories continue to change as we ask more questions and look closer. We once thought the earth was flat! Our awe and wonder asked us to dig deeper, to find more, to know more, and to share it. As we roll in orbit around our burning sun, we know that nothing is certain, and it's our awe that keeps us interested in the great mystery.

In Awe

I hear the jackhammer in the distance.
Someone is making something with skill and strength!
I see a single palm tree, leaning in thirst. How has it lasted?
It seems to have the face of an old woman in its bark.
The breeze carries the scent of saltwater
and I tune into four different bird calls at once.
One is a hummingbird. *I can hear it!*
The crows wake me up. It's spring and all
new growth can't help but point toward the light.

EXERCISE for FINDING AWE

CLOSE YOUR EYES AND POINT IN ANY DIRECTION

When you open your eyes, what's the first object you see? Is it a street sign? Is it a tree? Is it a photo of someone you love? Is it a sandwich? Whatever it might be, I ask you to be in awe of it.

How do we wake up the awe inside of us? Start by asking yourself who, what, why, where, when, and how. Who made the street sign? Who first touched it, who cut its shape, who designed it, who decided what it means? What kind of tree is it? What do you think about the color of its leaves? What feeling does it inspire inside of you when you see it? Why do you have this photo of someone you love in a frame? Why are they so important to you? Where did you buy the bread for this sandwich? Where did the wheat grow that the farmer used to make the flour? When did you last think about farmers and the fact that our food grows from the ground? How do you feel when you focus on the specifics that make up the world around you? A poem exists in this list of wonder. All of these questions and particulars add up, and the sum is poetry.

Drinking Water

I stand in the kitchen at night and revere the water.
I know it's a continuous traveler—down the drain
into the creek, rising into ether, moving toward the river,
the coastline, into the enormous ocean and back again.

I consider its archaic loop
as moonlight abruptly floods the room.

I worship the moon, marvel at illumination
so devoted to a cycle, so steadfast
it decides which way the swells should form
and guides the tides like a mother ushers
her child's legs into a garment.

Now I feel earth's orbit and sense
the magnitude of the universe,
only to turn off the tap and sip
from an unadorned clay cup.

WRITING PRACTICE

HOW TO MAKE A POEM
OUT OF AWE

Take out your journal, get situated at your desk with your computer, or write in this book—whatever's most comfortable for you. When you sit down to write, focus on something that inspires awe. Maybe it's the vastness of our oceans, or perhaps it's the small dragonfly on the kitchen windowsill. Start here, and let all of the questions you have about this subject matter come to the surface. Write each thought, no matter how disjointed. Let it be a rambling list of imperfections and delightful attributes, an inventory of the unknown below the ocean's surface, a catalogue of fascination that arises just by looking at the dragonfly's wings. You don't need to try very hard to find something to write about. The source of your idea might be a subject truly commonplace. It could be the pitch in your neighbor's laugh, the way your front door is shaped with a curve of quality redwood, or the giant brilliance of the moon rising. Let awe find you in a singular detail. Attach this mighty feeling to a string of thoughts, and then write about it all freely. Fill up at least a page, and don't worry about editing just quite yet. This loose paragraph of inspired language could end up a rough draft for a poem. Awe is meant to overflow, and if we let it arrive on paper, we'll be able to see it all around us that much more clearly.

Kneecaps

Overturned teacup bone
hidden under smooth
appeatance, how it bends
to bring us further,
great offering
of inner-workings
that show us what share
we have in fragility
and strength, what purpose
lies just below
the surface. Curve
and crook of walking
wonder, joint arranged
in gentle equilibrium
to carry us onward.

Housemates

Pierre Talón lives
in the kitchen,
close to the kettle
with an invisible web.
His brothers and sisters
share the same name.
Long glass-like legs
and dark teardrop bodies.
Penelope is on the front porch,
blending with the potted plant,
her green abdomen longer each day,
her hind legs like mechanical armor.
Pierre Talón catches the flies
and Penelope reminds me
to pause, peering between blossoms.
The spider never leaves, just changes
corners and sizes, and dodges the steam
when I make tea. The grasshopper
greets me for months, until one day
she sheds her skin and leaves me
with a perfect paper version of herself.

Nascar

Looped track of tradition,
just the sound alone
is proof that we endure
to enjoy togetherness
balanced with speed.
The engine of our
human design says
a circle of practice
pushing for glory
is ours to celebrate
as we call loudly
in the direction
of car after car,
all set in motion
to wow us
round and round again.

journal

What inspires your sense of awe?

POETIC MINDSET TIP

YOUR AWE CAN BE CONNECTIVE

Try applying a mentality of awe when you're interacting with someone who lives a life very different from yours. Let your awe be the inspiration for a connection. How did they come to believe something that makes you so uncomfortable? What is the root of their behavior? Maybe this person has a dissimilar political view. Maybe they live in a rural town, and you live in a city. Maybe they grew up practicing a particular religion, and you didn't. These are the big facts that surround the difference between you, but maybe this contrast can be intriguing instead of off-putting? When I find myself on a disparate page from someone else, I try not to close up. I try to lean in to discovery. It's frequently these occasions that surprise me the most and give me new insight.

When I let myself stay curious about another person's point of view instead of shutting down, I'm challenged to see with a new lens—and that feels creative. What would I have overlooked if I hadn't led with a sense of reverential respect? For example, through Poem Store, I developed very unlikely friendships that are still a huge part of my life.

From a familial bond with a timber baron to a deep camaraderie with a wealthy businessman, I found myself open to all kinds of folks I might normally shut out if I weren't in the mode of poetic openness.

Poetry helped us bridge the gap and see where our contrasting ideas actually overlapped in themes of family, love, trust, inventiveness, and hope.

These relationships continue to teach me how to develop compassionate language and an availability for dialogue that focuses on similarities, respect, and humanity, as opposed to difference, disdain, and judgment.

Letting your interest in a person's inner world outweigh your differences could have unifying results. Awe is often the key to the similarities we all share. It's our curiosity that links us, and these connections can cause the largest transformations.

chapter 2

MAKE MEANING

I have always believed, and I still believe, that whatever good or bad fortune may come our way we can always give it meaning and transform it into something else.

—HERMANN HESSE

One of the most incredible things about being human is the fact that we're able to appoint our own definitions and explanations for existence. We can base our interpretations on logical science, on dreamy mysticism, or even on gut instinct. Because we're the ones asking questions and finding answers, we're the ones who get to determine the meaning that we live by.

MEANING IS
A CHOICE.

It's a fascinating process because I know that I'm the one who adds significance to what is otherwise meaningless. This is the incredible skill of the human mind. We use our personal sets of data, balanced with our access to information, and nominate what we deem most meaningful. The trick is to fully be aware of your choices. This awareness of preference will enable you to respect the infinite possible designs of meaning that make sense for others. My meaning is wholly unique when held up next to yours, and the potential for my meaning to grow and shift is endless.

What's valuable to you isn't random; it's a crafted lens that you see through, that you add to and take away from willingly, throughout your lifetime.

You can delve into the details surrounding you and measure the might of sacredness in each. You can make the street sign sacred if you want to. Anything can be holy. When someone says over and over that they believe the rose quartz signifies unconditional love, it starts to hold this charge and is defined by it. We choose talismans that hold the power of our repetition. This repetition creates significance.

For me, a pencil is holy. I've assigned great meaning to the object, so that whenever I see one on my desk or discarded on the sidewalk, my eyes nearly well up. I find it to be the perfect balance of useful and beautiful, simple and purposeful. I have a pencil tattooed on my forearm. I choose to see it as a sacred object because I'm a writer, because I feel so moved by the creation of something that helps humans put words on a page, because I appreciate sleek, utilitarian design, and because I want to give the pencil consequence instead of just using it as an object that I don't notice.

Pencil

Functional form held
between my fingers,
you cast spells
in thin lines on paper,
soft sentences as grey
as sky that holds
a promise of storms rising.
How I need you and you're
there, easy answer
of yellow and earthly
contribution, graphite
gesture to make my mind
a thing seen in symbol.
Let me put my voice into
letters as you linger over
the page, prayers pouring
forth in my rambles that
you so generously shape.

EXERCISE for making meaning

PICK UP A COMMONPLACE OBJECT AND GIVE IT MEANING

Go to your kitchen. Pick up a spoon. Hold it in your hand and look at it. What is the first thing that it makes you think of? What is the first word that comes to mind? Does it offer you a memory? Does it connect you to something ancient and human? If you look at it and think, *This is just a spoon that I use to eat soup,* that's fine. But I bet you can notice more. Where did this spoon come from? Where did you buy it? Why did you choose it? Do you like eating with it? Is it too small or too big? How long do you think humans have been using spoons? Is a spoon sacred in any other culture? How can a spoon be sacred? Apply this exercise to any object in your home and suddenly you'll see that everything holds so much meaning. Start writing these personal definitions down and see the value that's already overflowing in the commonplace. This is the infinite collection of meaning that surrounds you.

WRITING PRACTICE

CREATE YOUR PERSONAL MYTHOLOGY

If we want to saturate our lives with meaning, we can create our very own mythologies to carry with us wherever we go. The way we do this is by assigning importance and definitions to objects and symbols. This is a very old human practice. Think of five things that are undeniably significant to you. Let's say you choose family, home, love, fun, and health. Now, assign an object or a symbol to represent each of these things. Family can be connected to the black bear because when you're all together you're like a family of bears, cozy in their winter den. Home can be connected to the sycamore tree because there is a giant one in the front yard. Love can be symbolized by a red heart. Fun can be the image of a mountain because you love climbing and that's your place for fun. Finally, health can be symbolized by the sun because when you're warm and bright, you feel most vital.

The bear, the sycamore, the red heart, the mountain, and the beaming sun. These are your symbols that you can carry everywhere with you and expand upon in writing. For example, take the black bear.

Why do you like it? What meaning comes up when you think about it? Do some research; find out what this animal means in your culture. Pull together the aspects that move you most and write your own definition. What words do you associate with this creature? What does it look like? This will highlight a personal, poetic importance for you, so that every time you see this animal or think of it, an intimate meaning will arise. This same practice works for plants as well.

No matter where you are, you have access to a mythology that applies to your personal narrative. This gives greater meaning to your reality and can be very helpful in the midst of hardship or uncertainty. These symbols, together or alone, can remind you that who you are is built on a large foundation of potent meaning.

At Home

Standing at the base of the sycamore,
the whole story of familial love
circles us in dappled shade.
We've come down from the mountain,
carrying joy deep in our red hearts,
sharing it as the sun flickers
over our faces. Eyes lifted
toward the leaves, a sense
of satisfaction is steady
as the seasons, sturdy
as the bear who walks the trail
somewhere near the ridgeline
named after our very own kin.

There are many animals and plants that help me navigate the world. I'm always alert, noticing which creatures cross my path, which plants are blooming when, so that I can interact with the symbols of my mythology as much as possible. This practice supports my mental health and adds a wealth of importance to my life. When I see a hawk, I'm reminded that I'm at home anywhere. When I'm at the beach and I see a dolphin surface, I'm reminded of my wisdom and freedom. When I see mugwort growing by a stream, I call it my friend and its silver leaves remind me of my dreams. When I see equisetum growing in the forest, I'm reminded how old the earth is, and I settle into a state of deep respect. Strung together, my assortment of consequence is a bountiful book of meaning that I can access whenever I desire a restored sense of connection.

Everything around you can have a lore attached. You can create a story of what it means to you. This can be applied to anything. To holidays, to cooking, to colors, to doing the laundry. It can hold importance if you say so, if you imagine it, and each aspect of your lifestyle can weave into an intricate mythology of purpose.

The Hawk and the Owl

For hawk I allocate the sign
of home. Whenever I see your red tail
in flight, I can feel the safety
of belonging, and you live almost
everywhere, so everywhere is my place.
Owl connects to omen, be it hard
or soft, the lesson that comes
with night eyes and hollow hooting
is one that says: pay close attention,
here is a moment of change,
a warning to look closer,
to take heed of bird's deep knowing.

Heart Rock

On the bank of the Trinity River
I find a heart shaped rock,
perfectly smooth
with a big scar in the center.
I used to fill my pockets with treasure:
pebbles, shells, bones and bark.
Now I just hold each one
and put it back where
it came from, a prayer
to remain in place.
But this worn stone,
with its distinct injury slightly
shining in the sun, comes home
with me. It sits in the center
of my altar and I coddle it
every morning. I cup it gently
and it exists as a unruined symbol
of ongoing work, the might
of mending that is left
in my hands alone.

What symbols, creatures, or objects
hold significance for you?

POETIC MINDSET TIP

KEEP YOUR MEANING UP TO DATE

Meaning helps us pay closer attention and take care of the world around us. Meaning is what makes everything matter. I'm in awe of the new meaning that humans create daily, as well as the ancient meaning that we cannot seem to shake. Meaning is personal, it's individual, and it becomes collective. It's our job to refine our own beliefs so that our actions carry the force of all our nuance, the power of our educated preferences, and the tone of our unique perspectives. Through the poetry of making meaning, we're illuminating personal and shared mythologies that inspire us all to be better humans, showing one another how to benefit from the complexity of consciousness. It's important that we put in the effort to refresh the things that we deem significant, to update our values as we change and grow, because this is the source of our selfhood and we're not fixed beings. The more we craft and collect meaning, the more we reshape and rebuild our points of reference, the wider the reach we develop, the more we understand, and with greater understanding comes greater possibility for opportunity, success, togetherness, and resolution.

chapter 3

Explore your Purpose

*I will serve the earth
and not pretend my life could be
better served.*

—WENDELL BERRY

any years ago, I was sitting on a rooftop in Oakland at a permaculture meeting. Surrounded by urban gardeners and farmers, the sunset casting a gorgeous pink across the sky, we listened as an elderly man began to discuss the beginning of his journey growing food and planting gardens. The first thing he said was, "You have to ask yourself this very important question: What do I serve?" He went on to say, "Some people serve God, some people serve themselves, some serve their community. It's okay if you can't answer this question yet, but I suggest you come back to the question every day until you can." I looked at him, his long white beard, the clouds like cotton candy swirling behind him, and I knew my answer immediately.

WHAT DO i SERVE?
i SERVE THE EARTH.

Everything I do as a poet, all of the energy I put into helping people through verse, it's all fueled by my hope to preserve the planet. I figure, if I help people find clarity, if I help them become more aware of beauty, more appreciative of the infinite bounty that surrounds them on a daily basis, then they'll in turn become better and treat the earth better. I love planet Earth. It's such a perfect gift, and I aim to do everything in my power to help protect it. This is my purpose.

It's okay not to know your purpose. A lot of people don't, although I believe it's there inside waiting to be identified.

Your purpose can change over the years. Your purpose can look clearly like something, and then you realize there's a hidden door to another aspect of intention that offers up new motivation. Maybe you have a few different types of motivation that fuel your existence, and all of these reasons for doing what you do can come out in small ways and large ways.

I'm Here

The city doesn't require me
to have a purpose.
It says I never need to think about
what I'm offering the world.
The essence is money.
The rest can be a blur
of hiding from the sun
in air-conditioned rooms.
No need for any of it to be holy.
Throw cups away, ten a day.
A cool night wind blows my window open.
I disagree with the mantras of this place.
I can't forget that I'm standing
on a planet that is floating in space.
I can't ignore my constant awe
or the words that arrive
while I'm sleeping. Each verse
written in the dark is a reason,
a reminder that I'm here
and I know why.

EXERCISE for Exploring purpose

DISCOVER THE PURPOSE OF YOUR FAVORITE WRITERS

Writers and artists create their work for a reason. Whether it be to simply let all of their emotions out onto the page so they don't explode, to inspire social change and activism, or to help heal their readers by sharing the guidance and wisdom of their personal story. There are countless reasons to write, and knowing why your favorite writers are or were dedicated to their craft can be helpful as you hone your own purpose.

For example, I'm so inspired by the way Audre Lorde speaks on behalf of intersectional feminism and civil rights in her poetry. Following her work, I'm able to witness how she chose to process her anger and use it to educate her readers.

This practice will require some research into the personal lives of the creators you look up to. You could read a memoir or simply delve into their body of work. Make a list of writers you share a common purpose with or a list of writers who you aspire to connect with creatively. We can often discover a writer's purpose from the arc of their career and focus.

How did they begin to write? Who's their audience? As their career progressed, did they attach themselves to a movement or a goal? Note their struggles, how they wavered or expanded, and think about your path of expression and what you want to do with the power of your words.

```
              Pathways

      Each mind is an offering
      of stairs, a structure
      of unique guidance,
      magnetic grace to ᴈ revise
      our route and aim us
      toward a higher realm.
      We do not move alone, our
      alignment allows for
      exploration, reveals new
      pathways designed by
      spirit and imagination.
      See here the steps are
      sturdy, we craft them
      wholly for each other.
```

WRITING PRACTICE

CREATE A POEM OF PURPOSE

I invite you to find your purpose by writing your thoughts about why you do the work you do, why you practice whatever activities you practice, and why you study whatever you study. This list can start with something very simple, such as you do your work for your family, you practice piano to relieve your mind after a busy day, and you study French because you want to go to Paris next year. But after these simple sentiments come forth, I urge you to look further. Why do you serve your family, why do you seek relief for your mind, and why do you want to travel to France? You may sit down every morning to write in your journal in an attempt to find out more about your inner world, but why do you want to know more about your inner world in the first place?

What are you doing to support something greater than yourself in the universe? Are you creating something to help alleviate suffering? Are you working to figure yourself out so that you can offer a whole version of your spirit to those around you? Are you doing any of this while you write? There are all types of purpose, and each one is crucial for our work as writers, but also for our work as humans in general.

As you figure out your purpose, you might also ask yourself who you are writing for. When I was in college, a writing professor asked each person in our class to consider: Are you a poet just for yourself? Do you want to show your writing only to your friends? Maybe you wish to write only for a tiny group of readers who like esoteric prose? Or maybe you want to write for everyone and anyone?

By answering this question, you allow yourself to find your voice. If you're writing for just yourself, you don't need to think twice about what comes out because it doesn't have to make sense to anyone but you. If you want to write for others, you have to think about accessibility and how to edit your work to be sure you're showing all that needs to be shown for widespread comprehension.

Who are you writing for? It's a helpful question that can unleash a freedom if you're making private work or inspire discipline if you wish to write something more universal.

I made the choice to write for everyone and anyone. I've always wanted my work to be fully accessible. My poetic purpose has solidified and widened over the years. I'm moved by the core consideration of doing everything for the earth and have elaborated on what that can mean. One night, while meditating on why I do what I do, the following poem flowed out onto the page. It's this kind of list that I'd like you to write for yourself now.

You can be vague and universal, or you can be immensely specific and personal. Just try and ask yourself why you want to write, what you think your voice has to offer, and let this offering be enough no matter how unassuming or bold.

My Poetic Purpose

To create relief.
To offer support.
To give alternatives.
To conjure compassion.
To reveal clarity.
To be selfless in service.
To show acceptance.
To assume responsibility.
To be an endless well, a mirror, and an outlet.
To hold space for healing.
To remain present and remember the wide reach
of our shared suffering.
To consider my duty.
To make and remake meaning.
To take care.
To provide deep connection.
To see the common link.
To shine a light on similarities.
To let our story show us how.
To hand over my voice.
To steer us all toward ᴢᴍ awe.
To sacrifice my agenda when new truth is made known.
To bring the depths to the surface.
To do worthy work, with grace.
To question and develop my intentions.
To honor life in any form.
To renew fᴏʀɢɪᴠɴᴇss forgiveness.
To try and be kind.
To try and be gentle.
To let my fire loose when it needs to be let loose.
To believe that rebirth is constant.
To revere, collect,and display the details.
To define beauty again and again.
To point out solutions.
To suggest the highest power.
To refine our definitions.
To present pure purpose.
To craft answers in lyric.
To remain humble and willing.
To rest and revive.
To expose the source.
To share the wisdom.
To listen and respond.
To uncover our abilities.
To find the bright part in every being.

To rejoice openly.
To witness the worst pain and find a lesson in it.
To open myself wider and wider.
To do the work in public.
To bring forth the language of the earth.
To honor my own effort.
To make an example of my devotion.
To let it often be hard and dark,
To cast out that which is not needed.
To give up many comforts in the name of logic.
To stand as a steward.
To weave a sturdy link between us and our place.
To display the significance in any little thing.
To never forget about the body.
Or underestimate the mind.
Or neglect the spirit.
To cry and howl and break.
To freely reimagine the best way to be.
To delve into the fearful areas.
To withstand the mistakes we keep making.
To bring enthusiasm.
To nurture transformation.
To love limitlessly.

What do you serve?

What is your poetic purpose?

POETIC MINDSET TIP

HOLD ON TO YOUR PURPOSE
ALL DAY LONG

Finding our purpose on and off the page is a long and winding road that asks us to dip into many facets of our character, interests, and passions along the way. Knowing your purpose is synonymous with knowing who you are. This is a lifelong human expedition, and if we can learn to check in with our intentions and motivations throughout the day, we can better understand who we are and what we need to thrive.

You don't just need to find your clarity of purpose as a writer; it's a mindset that affects your whole life story.

Just as you can add meaning to anything, you can add purpose too, and any purpose is valid. So, your job might seem somewhat uninspiring and tiresome, but if you're constantly checking in with your purpose for working there (for example, to support your family, to fuel your dreams as a painter, to receive great health benefits so that you can take care of your body and in turn savor adventures around the globe), then you can find an ongoing spark that adds justification to your daily endeavors. This is a mental practice that involves a ritual of reminders, the consistent appreciation for why you do what you do and why it matters.

The moment we let go of our purpose, our own worth can go away with it. So, holding on to purpose is in turn a radical act of self-preservation. As the weight of the world never lightens, loving yourself and upholding a persistent mantra of purpose can be a poetic gesture of wellness and joy.

chapter 4

SHARE your ANSWERS

Everything she said was like a secret voice speaking straight out of my own bones.

—SYLVIA PLATH

We all want to know more. Humans crave knowledge. As we explain ourselves through language, as we express the distinctions between our senses, as we collect images and explore them on the page, we're illuminating others by sharing our perspectives.

Show us the magic of this planet with your words. Show yourself the gorgeousness that surrounds you every day, and ask yourself, why is it so stunning? What about the view of the mountains moves you? Why is the color of her eyes so striking? Why is that song so arresting?

I love to keep asking why as I write. I sometimes discover a mysterious answer, sometimes a very concrete and logical one, but the question itself always prompts some newness in my work. For example, this is the epigraph at the beginning of my book of poetry *The Edge of the Continent Volume One: The Forest*:

Why do you love the forest so much?
It's my home.
How do you know it's your home?
It's the only thing my eyes want to see.

I not only ask the questions but also share the answers. Even when they're wholly personal, there is a chance that my findings will resonate with someone else simply because I'm human too.

I have a theory about this deep-rooted human desire to share. When something significant occurs, let's say when I see an eagle flying above me, the moment is that much more special if I can share it with someone else. I'm a huge fan of solitude for thinking and self-restoration, but when I delight over the wonders of life, I'm compelled to share them, to give them to someone else in the hope that they'll be just as or more inspired than I am. I give the moment to them through poetry, and therefore, I honor the moment by sharing it.

This is poetry: it's an exchange of moments, an offering of answers, a place where others can join in the lesson of wonder.

I often think about the way other writers have helped me out of my darkest places with their words. By sharing their work, they show me their approach to dealing with the pain of living and their connection to sorrow that's so similar to mine. I read their words and think, *Wow! If these writers, these fantastic creators, hadn't offered up their view, I wouldn't make it through this life.* And so I choose to do that work as well. We're all pulling each other through and healing one another by sharing our depths.

> *There is so much to be found in the dark,*
> *and when we sing about it, when we make*
> *a poem out of it, when we communicate*
> *about it all, that's how we transform it.*
> *We make use of it to the best of our ability,*
> *and it becomes beautiful. It becomes new.*

Through the poets and artists who suffered and shared, I've learned how to better embrace and understand my own suffering, along with humanity's suffering, and I've figured out how to let it all open me even further.

The Great Command

The great command holds
my attention at various points
throughout the day and night.
Keep on living, keep on living, keep on living.

I hear a voice ask me what abilities
can I manage, of what am I able?
I respond with
whatever I can muster.
I follow up my ideas with infinite thanks.
What else is there
in the face of such mystery
other than continuous celebration?
I'm just happy to be anything at all.

I say yes without fault
for nothing could be too wrong–
everything is as it should be.
How could it not be?

Equally, as others write about their great pleasures and triumphs, I find myself turning toward whatever source supplied them with such exuberance. The same goes with ancient texts about traditions, belief systems, and sacred practices. To read about the ways in which humans have celebrated being alive along the arc of time is to uncover ancient inclinations that live within me. This informs my process and enriches not only my historical knowledge but also my personal mythology, which uplifts all that I do.

I'd like to point out here to be very mindful of cultural appropriation. I'm not suggesting we all take freely from other cultures and announce ownership over what feels best for us. I'm advocating for an individualized exploration that is private. I'm an amalgamation of all that resonates with me spiritually, artistically, and aesthetically, and I wouldn't know how to rise into the wholeness of my story without having access to the shared stories of others. But at the same time, I do my best to honor each and every fine line that exists between my sacred practices and the origins of my inspirations.

EXERCISE for SHARING

READ ALOUD TO OTHERS AND SHARE YOUR WORK

One great way to understand the importance of sharing is to read aloud. Share your own writing or poems by your favorite poets with a friend or a loved one. See what happens as the words are expressed out loud.

> POETRY IS AN ORAL TRADITION, AND READING IT TO ONE ANOTHER CAN BE TRANSFORMATIVE.

When I write poems for people, I always read them aloud. Their retention level is higher because they can hear the inflections and cadence in my voice, and all of this says just about as much as the words themselves.

Even better than reading aloud is sharing your printed work while reciting it. Your friend can listen to you read as they follow along on the page. Sharing your work in progress is a great way to get feedback, but it doesn't have to feel like a workshop or editing practice. You can simply ask the listener to take in your words without any criticism. Sometimes it's helpful to hear yourself share, to witness someone else encountering your work, and this act of participation can provide just enough vulnerability to ignite new inspiration.

WRITING PRACTICE

HOW TO EDIT YOUR WORK FOR SHARING

In order to share more effectively, it's important to learn how to edit and adjust our writing. When we write, we're trying to discuss existence through our own exceptional eyes, and it's hard to find a balance between the preciousness of the personal and the crafting of clarity for our readers.

After I write a first draft, I start the editing process by finding the places in the poem where I'm telling the reader something without including an image or sensorial addition that enhances what I'm trying to relay. How can I add a bit of definition to something mysterious? How can I include my reader in a very metaphysical opinion?

This is where the technique "show, don't tell" comes into practice. Instead of telling the reader what the bird singing on my windowsill looks like, I try to explain its song and feather coloration with metaphor. I try to avoid clichés by connecting the bird to something unexpected.

Here's an example of how to move
from the telling to the showing:

Why just tell us this?

The wonder of this day
is the dove
in the morning.
The sun rises
and it flies
with white wings.
It is beautiful
and small, moving
higher as I start
another day.

When you could show
us this:

The wonder of this day
is the fringed white wing
of the dove as it flies
east toward the rising
sun–– first light
caught in its laced
flight, a lady's glove
taken by wind, its coo
a delicate voice
that reminds me:
I am indeed
beginning again.

Can you see the difference? If you're writing about your daughter's first visit to the ocean, show us the expression on her face. Compare it to something personal, something that someone else can relate to, something unlike any other thing, because your daughter's face is unlike any other thing on earth.

This is the delicate work of word choice, and it's a huge part of the craft of poetry that takes a lot of practice. Choosing the right word isn't something that necessarily comes naturally. It's an exercise that may get easier over time, and it's as connected to a writer's confidence in voice as it is to the ability to see beyond their own lens.

If I'm trying to invite anyone and everyone into my work, that doesn't mean I use simplified language. Instead, I have to build a language that is both uncommon and understandable.

When I edit my work, I circle words that feel trite or ordinary, and I do my best to avoid anything too abstract. The words *love, fear, hate,* and *beauty* are huge words that mean something very different to every single person, and they're abstractions. If you want to tell your readers about love and fear, write out your very own vulnerable version. What kind of love is it that you want to share? What does fear feel like in your body? Find something exact and strange to evoke an extremely distinct image for the reader, who wants to follow your special lead and see something they never thought to notice about love, fear, hate, or beauty. It's our job as writers to add to these abstractions and make them our own.

Here's an example of addressing
an abstraction:

Why just tell us this?

I feel love
in my heart
when you come over.
My tears stop,
sadness leaves me,
and I am no longer
lonely, just happy
and held close.

When you could show
us this:

This electric feeling
is the universe saying
yes, bright spark
in the center of my chest,
fever rising from
a dream. You arrive
in the doorway and I am
suddenly awake, thriving
on your dark eyes,
drinking your gesture
of open arms.

When you write, which words do you use again and again? Spend some time making a list here, and try to flesh them out, add meat to their trite bones, apply new definitions to their old descriptions. Work your words. When I find a word that feels kind of clunky or overused, I look it up in the thesaurus, following the lead of language page after page, click after click. Write down words you haven't heard before and use them in your work. Dive into language like it's a treasure hunt. This is my favorite way to reinvent the wheel as I write, to redesign my feelings in a way that's accessible and different for my readers. It's also just so much fun to explore the vast reservoir of words.

Grant yourself permission not to know
every definition and to discover
newness every time you write.

journal

Work your words:

POETIC
MINDSET TIP

LET ACCESSIBILITY BE THE INSPIRATION IN ALL COMMUNICATION

The reason for all of this exactness is plain and simple: accessibility. We all want to be understood, and even if we aren't trying to write poems for everyone, we can work through our thoughts and make them easier for someone else to understand before we communicate them. This can be inspiring for all types of connection. When we ask a person we love for something difficult, a needed change in behavior, a request for honesty or appreciation, having our language come across as comprehensible and clear is really important. This is the art of poetic editing. Are you sharing to the best of your ability? Can you consider applying some tools first so that when you speak or write you're being as intelligible and as approachable as possible? This practice can reconstruct our ability to relate to one another, to connect on a deeper and more efficient level. A friend once called me a radical communicator. I loved this and attribute my communication skills to my poetic mindset. My ability to speak clearly and fully comes from my consistent engagement with language and the fact that I believe each word carries great importance.

chapter 5

USE your SENSES

But poetry is a portal through which we glimpse the shimmering inner core of sentience itself.

—PAUL BROKS

With any one of our senses, we can uncover a wealth of inspiration. I smell the blooming jasmine and let it spark a memory of my first visit to Los Angeles, and then a poem begins to form. I touch a soft shirt in the back of my closet that belongs to an ex-partner and am shocked into the pain of that time period, only to write a tribute that re-creates the love I once felt for that person and affords me some new closure. I hear a melody and suddenly compare the high-pitched sound of the violin to my outrage over the current political climate. I taste a bite of key lime pie and my entire childhood unravels in the flavor, revealing the power the body holds over our experience. All of these connections create space for self-reflection, remembrance, and clarity, which is helpful when I might otherwise be having a hard time locating beauty or happiness.

My senses are innate tools that reveal grandeur in the ordinary if I choose to use them this way, and they wake me up to the plentiful splendor that surrounds us all.

I like to move through each one of my senses to discover what they expose. This can be like a game of finding the silver lining, as I choose to let each sense illuminate something positive or profound. It's my way of letting my imagination be an active thing that expresses itself through my body, sense by sense.

When I hear something, the nature of sound waves can wow me, the thing I hear can move my spirit. Just a note can express passion or sorrow. Each sound carries its own influence. The traffic outside my door is a calming white noise. The muffled voices of my neighbors make me nostalgic for childhood, when my parents would have a dinner party while I was falling asleep in the next room.

When I smell something, I'm taken backward in time. The geranium makes me think of my grandma, and I can suddenly access the unconditional love she gave me. The nasty stench of hot garbage makes me long for an incredible summer I once spent in New York City.

When I taste something, I'm taken to landscapes I've yet to visit. This tin of delicious mackerel transports me to the Spanish coast. The flavor of this tiger nut is so new, like nothing I've ever tasted, and I have to find unique words to describe its sweetness.

When I touch someone, or something, so much information passes through my fingertips. I process some of it, but if I pay closer attention, I might access a trauma or a joy that only touch can create. My hand on another person's hand helps me delve into our connection. My hand on an old piece of redwood aids my recollection of climbing trees in Northern California.

When I see something beautiful, I can simply write down what I see, and revisiting that image later is soothing, comforting, and expansive because I can ask myself, Why is it beautiful? How can my eyes see such dimension, such color, such detail? And with this, I'm standing in awe again.

I Can Stay

Only the strong scent
of blooming citrus
and the sound of banana leaves
moving in the wind
can save me tonight.

I got lost,
got a parking ticket
and I feel lonely.
There is nothing
anyone could say
to heal me.

I pass by your porch.
The garden that isn't mine.
Plants call out for water.
I stick my finger
into each pot
to search out their thirst.

If I walk down the saddest
sidewalk and find
the magnolia in bloom
then in the city I can stay.

It is blooming.
Giant saucers of white.
I dig my fingernails
into the thick, fallen petals.

EXERCISE for THE SENSES

HEIGHTEN AND APPRECIATE YOUR SENSES

Focus on one sense today. My friend once did an experiment like this trying to heighten each sense, listening closely to the sound of his cat breathing, putting his face into a bowl of freshly cut flowers, eating a very spicy chili, rubbing his muscles with oil after a hot shower, indulging each of his senses in a new way. Try some version of this and write down your sensations, connecting the dots to memories, lingering in newness, and trying to assign innovative language to each sensual event. What feels healing about this practice? What feels hard about it? Every one of these moments is a poem. Try a new sense tomorrow. Let it be poetic, and write down your reactions.

GETTING IN TOUCH WITH YOUR BODY OPENS A VAULT OF INFORMATION.

You're abundant with sensorial intelligence, and if you let it guide your pen, you might gain access to parts of your story that have been buried within you for some time.

WRITING PRACTICE

BRING AT LEAST ONE SENSE INTO EVERY POEM

To keep circling back to your senses, for the next few weeks as you write make sure to touch upon at least one sense in your work. Did you write a poem about going to the beach? Make sure you include a sensory expression. Did you write about a phone call with your mom? Try delving into the sound of her voice and what it felt like to hear her. Not every poem has to mention the senses, but it's a really good way to get your point across by demonstrating something and not just telling the reader about it.

Alongside Highway 299

Multiple chainsaws harvest
timber in the basin. The crack
of big doug fir bodies falling
one after another, trunks
pounding the earth like a drum.
No voice laments these endings.

Yet the insects do sing.
Summer birds variegate notes.
Leaves speak—the ones
that float unfixed
sound like paper unfolding,
the yellows catch light
and bring quick bright
words to the dark forest.

The highway is too close to my cabin—
loud clank of tractor-trailers
and groaning engines, brakes
yowling like angry cats
on the mountain incline.
This far into the woods
and I still have to sift through sounds
to find the pure voice of earth.

I walk the trail to the garden,
sticks splitting beneath my boots.
For months I thought the strange
call of the grouse was a generator.
Then early one morning I saw
his shaking feathers, his throat
taut with passion.

When the road falls into the ravine,
when most of us are gone, maybe
an old and hidden language
will resurface. Even now, it offers
hints of itself when I stand
alone in the quiet night.

My Name in Cursive

Just this morning I said aloud
I'd like it if you brought me flowers.
I unbraided my hair while running
downhill to the mailbox. Three horses
stood in the field across the street,
brown backs glowing golden in the sun.
Touching my hair while looking at them
mixed our soft warmth, somehow kindred.
I opened the box to find a red rose
taped to an envelope, my name
in cursive on the front.
It still smelled sweet enough
and I kissed the petals as a farmer
passed me in his moaning pickup truck.
I laughed the whole way back up
to the house and the crows cackled, too.

journal

Explore your senses:

POETIC MINDSET TIP

SHARPEN YOUR SENSES
AND HONE YOUR AWARENESS

Being in touch with our senses helps us with our overall awareness and perception. This enhanced skill of observation amplifies our poetry as we write, but it also adds to our general outlook as we become more in tune with the world around us through the sharpening of our senses. If we let our senses guide us through our day, we discover the bounty of involvement that our body and mind undergo on a regular basis, often without our noticing. Focus on the sensual, and the mundane suddenly rises into the awestruck, as we easily pull from the sounds, scents, sights, tastes, and feelings all around us. It's quite healing to move through the day fully awake, realizing we're endowed with a natural ability to indulge in sensuality on so many levels. This practice always leaves me awash with gratitude. When I remember to concentrate on my senses, I'm conscious in an expansive way and capable of noticing so much more of the majesty that's constantly available to us all.

chapter 6

USE your PAIN

The state of the world calls out for poetry to save it.

—LAWRENCE FERLINGHETTI

*P*oems don't just create a shared understanding of awe or lead us into sensual wonderment, they also help us to uncover our pain and heal as we face the depth of our individual and collective ache. Poetry is therapy, whether you're reading it, writing it, or simply evoking it in thought patterns and perspectives. Through poetry we touch the places that are too painful to linger in, we sift through our feelings of trauma, and we expose ourselves to the fact that we are not alone in this hurt.

ARE you BROKENHEARTED AND ANGRY? THERE'S A POEM FOR THAT.

Here is the place, on the page, where you can let your inner fire burn as hot as you want, to witness it letter by letter, and to know it better. Shout each word aloud. Throw the page into the fireplace after you write. Seal your ramble in an envelope and tuck it away to revel in after you've found more healing. Just get your anger out, and let poetry be your container.

Are you mourning the loss of a loved one? Write a poem to let the pain loose.

You're a bottle that cannot hold the pressure of this sadness. Your grief truly needs nothing from you but gentleness, no matter how demanding it feels. Your process can be as slow as you like.

This is where a mantra of poetry can be of great assistance. Say a line over and over to remind yourself of what was beautiful about this person, what they taught you, what they left behind for you, and what work they're asking you to do in their absence. Single lines of clarity about life, death and loss, emptiness and pain, all of it can keep you company in your darkness, not as light perhaps, but as a part of the process.

Without You

It's your birthday
and all I can do is think
about your parents while looking
at this photo of you as a baby,
when you were new. Just learning air,
joyous and blank, free with the same
eyes, the same open look saying *yes*
to this weird life. Without you,
we celebrate the years you left us with,
a small chunk of time that overflows
with stories. You were a shining man,
always giving us a reason to rejoice,
and so you still are, you always will.

Are you misplaced and betrayed? There is a poem to soothe you. What are the words you use to soothe yourself? Can you expand upon them now?

What are the words you would use to soothe someone else? You're allowed to use these words for yourself. Put them down in writing and let them be of aid.

What would you wish your life to be like instead of what it is? Write it all down. Read it out loud. How does it sound? Does it show you where your wound resides?

The Relief of Our Endless Becoming

What is it that we're doing here?
Go ask the largest tree in sight.
It answers: We're just meant to make
and make, reaching toward the highest
place. It's all a guess, this growth,
this work. Someday we topple over, burn,
break, unfurl, and our particles
become another form. The black space
between stars, flesh and limb, rope,
rose, graphite, ~~arxbreath~~ grass
or breath, thére is always
something new for us to be.

There is nowhere else you need to be. Just here, lost, begging, beginning, asking, searching, saying yes to the truth of this adversity and knowing that you're not alone. Here, in this poetry, we accept the fact that it's hard to be alive.

Whenever my life gets unbearable and I ask my-self questions like *Why keep going? Why stay here at all? Why is life worth living?* I always circle back to my curiosity about the great mystery of exis-tence. How miraculous is it that the hardest things push us into rebirth? What is this wild and weird re-ality that we get to be a part of? The conundrum of the quest is itself a poem.

Throughout human history, we've used the suc-cinct power of poetry to unite our suffering. Poetry is at the helm as we navigate the horrors of war, the weight of political abuse, and the hardship of trauma. We still look to Homer's *Iliad* to process the causes of bloodshed, we read Pablo Neruda and explore his response to his country's political strife, and Sylvia Plath guides us through her personal pain.

It's poetry that rises as we process our grief—slow and steady songs of reality to hold us while we do the work of healing.

It Is Hard to Be Alive

It is hard to be alive.
Yet, beauty never goes missing,
there is always a deep
well somewhere, and even when
we feel we are fully without,
empty and done, the tides
keep talking to the moon,
every detail pointing toward
another possibility, toward
endless transformation.

Knuckle Tattoo

First I decided to stop in town
at the old house by the pasture—
I thought maybe you'd be there playing guitar
or curled up on the couch talking
about steel drums and parades. I parked in front
of what used to be my window, the room
where you taught me how to harmonize.

And the neighbor girl approached.
She said some semitruck
smashed you last night and now
all we have are your songs.

Your best friend stood at the kitchen sink,
your girlfriend wailed as I stroked her hair,
poured tea, built an altar.

This is when I tattooed my knuckles—
a nickname forever in ink
near bone to remind us
that even if we can sing in perfect pitch
we all leave this place
not knowing why or when.

EXERCISE for MAKING PAIN USEFUL

FIND THE SOURCE

This is a tender exercise, a tracing of pain, the path back to the deepest wound. For myself, a huge hurt that I carry is often the source of great realizations and growth. I've worked with many different types of therapy for years to figure out where my pain stems from, and my curiosity has been my greatest guide in this effort. I want to know why I am the way I am, and my trauma informs so much of my mindset. Do you know where your pain comes from? Does it point back to a certain occurrence? Do you have only a vague idea, a slight memory, that seems to be the source? What do you do to familiarize yourself with the hurt you carry?

In our writing, we can uncover the how and why of our pain, looking deeper into the process of its becoming, and then we can begin to dismantle it.

There are countless, well-trusted methodologies to help us become acquainted with our pain, and when we dig into this work, the cave of our understanding becomes incredibly deep.

I like to turn my pain into a guide. I follow its directions, meditating on where it all began. It's at these starting points where I find the most potent feelings. My heartbreak from a failed relationship will often give me a chance to let out my sadness in verse, but not before I try to unpack the whole story. Only when I attempt to understand the many aspects of this failed relationship can I fully feel it and pay tribute to it. I begin this kind of investigation by rambling in my journal. Then, if I feel inclined, I might pull the heart of my understanding into poetic form. I recently wrote a book of poetry called *Help in the Dark Season*, which focuses on my childhood trauma, the way it affects my adult relationships, and the modes of healing that have helped me grow. Writing this book was extremely hard, but after I finished, I felt like I'd turned coal into gold. I pulled back the curtain inside myself and let light do its thing. Now I not only get to feel the inner effects of my work but I'm also able to witness the importance of sharing this book with others, the way my words act as a key to unlock their personal process of healing. The result of this revealing has been an honesty and a newness that I couldn't have reached without the alchemy of writing poetry.

I urge you do to this hard work with your trauma, if you're able. Give yourself permission to move into the realm of blame. Maybe move beyond it toward forgiveness.

HOWEVER your process looks, you can write it down and find the poetry that pain presents.

Our traumas create our fears, and our responses to these fears can be as poetic and beautiful as we make them. Let your pain be a source of inspiration, turn this heavy load into poetry, own it, use it, and take as much from it now as it has taken from you in the past.

Close your eyes and meditate on the hidden ache you carry. I like to start with my childhood because that's what makes sense for me, but you can start anywhere along your timeline. Do you see any images attached to your discomfort? Can you try and put words to your grief and your loss? Who hurt you? What was their childhood like? Why did they do what they did? Make use of the pain of being alive. See the universality in whatever caused you harm, and focus on the connection to others who have survived similar experiences. When I sit with my wounds, I find my resilience, and that makes me want to linger there, gather up the lessons left in the aftermath, and use them for my own creation. Writing about my pain enables me to claim it as my own, and this ownership is empowering.

Every poem holds the power to do this healing work, to give a reflection, to present a relationship with newness and possibility.

How can you show your reader your personal methods of self-care in a poetic way? Maybe start by writing a list of poems or even song lyrics that have been healing for you in the past. I have poems dog-eared and underlined in every book on my shelf, and I'll pull them out in a moment of need. They're my reminders that yes, it is indeed hard to be alive for everyone.

WRITING PRACTICE

HOW TO WRITE A HEALING POEM

My work with Poem Store allowed me to witness humanity's widespread suffering. We're all aching over loss and dissatisfaction, over cruelty and hatred, and yet, when someone makes space for our pain, we find solace. In every spontaneous poem that I write in response to sorrowful subject matter, I make space for the pain. Each line I create shows the reader that I see them, I hear them, I accept their struggle and respond to it openly, with care and consideration. Just as I do this for others, we can all do this for ourselves through poetry as well.

How can a poem be healing? Add light to the dark places. Write down the ways your pain has been an impetus for positive change. My issue with feeling unlovable caused me to engage in a healing process that has allowed me to better express myself with friends and lovers, enriching my connections and communication skills. My pain actually opened me up.

Let the dark places be teachers.

Describe the lessons you've learned and the ways you've grown in response to the most hurtful parts of your life. Understanding that my childhood trauma affects my present relationships has enabled me to have compassion for myself and my behavior, which I might otherwise judge harshly. This compassion slows me down and helps me clearly communicate my needs.

Balance your pain with future possibility. Consider what it looks like to live with your pain and to accept the healing process for the long haul. After losing my best friend to drugs and alcohol, I see my grief as a continuation of our connection, a lifelong presence that will help me help others in the future.

Let the sorrow be compared to all things light and heavy. Does it burn hot like the sun? Is it an iron plate over your chest? When I envision my sorrow, I see my heart as a burnt charcoal rose with a hole in it. As I practice healing and write about my feelings, the rose changes shape; it sings and blooms according to my willingness to tend to it.

Heart Song II

I'm the white heron.
I'm the ginger root.

Wings wide in seamless
effort, floating high above.

Deep spice dug from soil,
built in darkness.

When I see my heart
it's a rose
made of charcoal.

The hole inside
is dark and the petals
wither around it.

But I spread my feathers
and my body dives down
into fire, where I remember—

The rose has a season
and look now, it's huge again,
pure red, singing within this small breast.

If you don't feel whole, try to write down a version of wholeness that makes sense to you. Use this practice as if it were a spell meant to call your wholeness into form. I like to meditate on the things I'm afraid of and then make a counter list, reversing my fears: I'm not afraid to be loved; I'm not afraid to ask for what I need; I'm not afraid to be the student. Then I like to flesh these ideas out and make poetry with the results. This is a recipe for my healing.

Remind your reader that we're all sad together. When they see your sadness on the page, it acts as a mirror. We're not meant to look away from suffering. It's a catalyst that leads to greater wisdom. Remind your reader that renewal is an innate human skill. We're made to grow and become better. Our bodies renew. Our minds renew. We heal and change. This is a truth built into being, and so, it can be built into our poems as a healing tool. Show us what it looks like to move from one state to the next; let us see your exploration and your struggle to become new. A poem can remind us of the methods we have access to that help us all recover.

A poem can say yes, this suffering is immense, but mending is an ancient art. Show yourself how you have mended before, how your ancestors healed, how humans always find a way to keep moving onward even in the face of great struggle.

Write about your healing journey.
What does your heart look like today?

POETIC MINDSET TIP

YOUR PAIN IS A SEED FOR GROWTH

These writing practices carry over into our quiet moments, into the dismal and dulling places of pain that keep us awash in forgetfulness, lacking inspiration. There's one thing to remember here, even when everything is too heavy for poetry: your pain is a seed for growth. From the worst ache comes the gift of newness. Heartbreak calls for mending, and then our form is forever altered. Instead of hardening around this change, we can embrace it, thankful for the wisdom that accompanies such transformation. In times of doubt, we can say, "My pain is a seed, my pain is a seed, newness is coming, newness is coming," and we'll never be wrong, no matter how long we take to root and flourish.

chapter 7

USE your MEMORIES

. . . lover, loser, red rose and ragweed,
these are the tracks I have left
on the white crust of time.

—MARGE PIERCY

I only know how to define certain things about myself, about my identity and beliefs, because I'm aware of my past. With this awareness, I've discovered repetitions and patterns, as well as concepts that come up again and again, always bringing intrigue and inspiration. I know what excites me and what motivates me to ask questions and dig deeper. All of this helps me understand myself better.

KNOWING MYSELF HELPS ME FIND HAPPINESS AND SUBJECT MATTER for WRITING.

This is all connected to the idea that we're formed by our childhoods. As base level and unimaginative as that may be, it's hard to deny that everything eventually leads back to what was. In therapy, this is often what transpires. We walk the path of the past to discover what happened to us, what made us so fearful or so angry. What life laws did we learn and tie into our cores at a young age? Why did certain things happen to us? Can we uncover the cause and effect? Why do we behave the way we do now? Our current character is linked to various aspects of our past. Are these links things we're aware of or not?

A lot of this work is positive. For example, why do I love pumpernickel bread? Because my grandmother covered it in thick pads of butter for me so many times when I was a kid. Why am I so drawn to farming and animal husbandry? Because my parents sent me to a farm camp, where I learned how to care for animals and grow vegetables. Why am I so quick to strike up deep conversation with people I hardly know? Because I watched my grandfather do this outside the grocery store every week.

Along with these sweet understandings are the harder aspects of the quest for self-knowledge through memory. I've figured these answers out in therapy and through writing poetry. I had some intense realizations as I discovered that I'd been operating from a place in the past, with information given to me by my parents, and that I no longer need to fall into these patterns. I can let that part go.

But if I hadn't been willing to dig in to the past in the first place, I never would've been able to put two and two together in the present, thus affecting my future. I struggle deeply with believing that I'm loveable. As someone who is both awestruck and blessed with many loving relationships, it can get confusing for me to understand why I feel this way. But when I look back into my past, at my childhood especially, I can see clearly the source of this loveless belief. My mother expressed to me, many times and in many different ways, her lack of love for me. My father did the same. I've worked hard to heal from this early hurt, but wounds like this are long-lasting. These wounds will supply me with endless information and motivation for healing, and this information can be spun into poetry as I give myself power and ownership over my pain.

How does the past affect our current behavior? It might not feel good to go back and relive memories, but there's usually some things we carry over into present relationships or in thought patterns that affect us here and now. If we don't look at them, how can we decide what to let go of and what to keep? Do we have character traits that arise simply because of the past? If we look closer, can we release these things once we see they're no longer of any use? Why do we act the way we do? The past can help us find reasons; it can show us our habits and remind us what the mind and body hold on to. The past can put up a red flag and signal all of the compulsions and ideas we need to shed or investigate more closely. This practice can be key to unlocking our transformation. It can guide us in our quest to piece together the complicated puzzle of the self, and this puzzle is a poem.

Why look into the past? Why see it as a map and make a record of our rambling timeline? Because the results fill us with the light of understanding. Now that I can see in my current state the shadow of my previous years, I can more rationally digest everything that makes me who I am. This is what I hope the practice will offer you; a method to help you clarify your background in a way that's illuminating, in a way that fills you with empowering appreciation and overwhelming acceptance.

The Task of Love

Lover, friend, family,
human with whom I share
this life--
May you always remember
my deepest wound and carry it
with you in every moment
so that my actions, be they
beast-like or softly tender,
are simply a signal for your
compassion. I define
my vulnerable self with this
hurt that speaks to you
in spitfire or sobbing,
and each time you love it
without question, I am
healed more and more.

No Siblings

It's not that I was born
on a sinking ship.
My parents abandoned me
on deck as if I were a wolf
with an oar in her mouth.
I learned how to swim,
jumped in after them
dragging our vessel behind me.
I can't stop hoping for a crew.
I have only this cup
with a dead spider in it
and a song about
how many times my mother
sold the family pet. Rip it all
from memory and no one
will stop me because clarity
is a pearl lost somewhere
in the silky folds
of a very deep purse.
I found the horizon, the place
where the sun hits the water.
Who will I show it to?

Nostalgia

How humans are able
to survive
and simultaneously
remember each and every
thing that has happened.
Ancestors in blood,
strange surge of emotion
in sense, this scent,
this color, the ghost
of this place alive
and well, each moment
heavy with a welcome
haunt and always
wowing us into awe.

EXERCISE
for memory

THINK OF ALL YOU'VE DONE
AND LET IT WOW YOU

Sit down with a blank sheet of paper, your notebook, or use the space in this book. Give yourself more than one session with this exercise. Sometimes looking backward takes a lot of energy. Be gentle with yourself. If we look back in time, we're able to follow a line of achievement and experience that can explain the present moment. This map can offer clarity where before there was only a blur. It can be a great exercise for presenting yourself with the bounty of your life, which you may have forgotten about. Start by answering the following questions. These are just a jumping-off point; keep writing your memories as they come to you.

Think of all you've done. The list will be endless, and everything adds up to show what an eventful and interesting life you've led. The answers can be elementary yet gratifying. After you answer these questions, you'll have a collection of subject matter. The poetry of your past can be the essence of your current creation.

What feelings come up when you read the word *past*?

What incident from your past was truly transformative?

What have you done in your life that you're proud of?

What have you learned?

What good deeds have left you with a feeling of fulfillment?

What have you made, built, designed, brought into being?

What jobs have you worked?

Have you had children?

.

Have you won any prizes or races?

Have you written any books?

Which books have you read?

Have you painted any paintings? Painted a house?

Have you fostered an animal in need?

Have you put in a kitchen sink?

What helped you shape your belief system?

What events caused you to trust in one thing and not another?

Have you gone to school?

Have you been in love?

Have you made a friend?

Have you seen something you thought was beautiful?

Has someone held you close while you cried?

Have you written a song?

Have you purchased a car?

Have you ridden a bike, swum in the ocean, completed a certification?

Have you eaten a delicious apple?

I learned how to ride a bike,
catch fish, snorkel, and drive a stick-shift.
I got a degree in poetry
and a minor in anthropology.
I swam in oceans, lakes, rivers,
creeks and sinkholes.
I've used a chainsaw, a nail-gun,
a glue-gun, a shotgun, and a pitchfork.
I've made paintings, drawings, clothes,
cakes, pies, pasta, songs, and videos.
I've served and bused tables, worked
on farms and ranches, tended goats
and mustangs, edited manifestos,
and harvested bull-rush seeds
for wetland restoration.
I've used an oven, a woodstove, a toaster,
a fire-pit, and a microwave.
I've danced, played music in bands,
done yoga, watched movies, and hiked up mountains.
I've fixed up cars, bikes, greenhouses,
chicken coops, and mended book bindings.
I've lived in cities, in the desert,
in the swamp, on an island and in the forest.
I've slept under the stars, on a cot,
on a sailboat, on the floor, in the car,
and in a king-size water bed.

WRITING PRACTICE

CREATE YOUR TIMELINE

I always say the past is a map. It's a collection of data showing us where we've been, what we've done, and who we are. My favorite part of using memory to catalyze poetic appreciation for existence is the following exercise. I decided to look back in time to find the things that made me feel, *Wow! If that's all I ever did in life, that was enough.* I wrote out a list of ten things I've done that fill me with gratitude. For example, I've driven across America more than ten times, I've written thousands of poems for strangers that I'll never see again, and I supported a friend struggling with a meth addiction. I wrote these experiences in my notebook and started drawing little graphs and maps of them. Then I moved on to a big piece of butcher paper to gradually draw an actual timeline starting from the day I was born.

You can begin with the year you were born, or the year you went to college, or the year your child was born—any point in time, really. You don't even have to write dates. Just make note of anything that felt important along the way. The wonder of reality adds up in our actions, past to present. This timeline is a poem. You can add to it for the rest of your days and see how it all combines to create your one-of-a-kind human story.

WROTE THIS BOOK

MADE MY LIVING AS A POET

2009 STARTED POEM STORE

LIVED OFF-GRID & GREW FOOD

RODE MY BICYCLE IN SOUTH AMERICA

BOUGHT MY FIRST CAR & DROVE ACROSS THE USA

GOT REALLY INTO PERMACULTURE

TRAVELED THE COUNTRY IN A NOISE BAND

MOVED TO VENICE FL FOR HIGH SCHOOL

HARDLY EVER TOOK OFF MY BATHING SUIT

MY MOM MOVED US TO THE FLORIDA KEYS W/ HER BOYFRIEND WAYNE.

LIVED IN 7 DIFFERENT HOUSES BY THE TIME I WAS IN 3RD GRADE. ONE HOUSE WAS ON A LAKE.

MOVED BACK TO HUMBOLDT

GOT FIVE BOOKS PUBLISHED

MOVED TO HUMBOLDT

LIVED IN SEATTLE

CERTIFIED IN PERMACULTURE

2010 GOT INTO FISH NET POETRY

WENT DIVE AND LIVED OUT IN A NOISE PARK

LIVED IN OUR OLD VAN OR A 360 OLIVE

PARENTS GOT THE ROYAL OAK BOAT

NOV 1984 HABITION IN ROYAL OAK MI

journal

Notes for your timeline:

Inspired by my timeline practice, I asked myself to think back to my very first memory, and that prompt inspired the following poem:

How I Fell in Love with the Earth

I don't remember being born,
but I did choose to come here.
A master in the dark,
my burning light.
I shot forth, hungry
for the ground and body.
After 34 years, I trace back
to my first moment of awe.
I stood above an overturned flagstone,
staring at long nightcrawlers
worming in black soil. Inhaling
each color, mesmerized by the chance
that brought these pink lengths to life.
Their tenderness against
a thick crust that welcomed
them into fissures, into fine versions
of string sucked toward the core,
roaming blind, becoming and becoming.
Everything else was unlit space,
green grass moving in the void.
I've witnessed enough.
What perfection to break my heart.

POETIC MINDSET TIP

LEARN HOW TO APPRECIATE THE PAST

What have you done that wows you? That makes you appreciate your life? So many small things come together to create the poem that is our existence, so many major events are ours to endure, starting the second we take our first breath. It's as simple as this: every time I revisit my past, I'm reminded of what a full life I've led, and even with all of the hardship, with the trauma and the hurt that come with memory, I still see this overflowing bounty behind me and end up feeling grateful to have experienced so much. Tapping into the past is a way to gain appreciation for the present, and if we can value who we are right now, we can consider our poetic selves and honor whatever it is we need to voice.

chapter 8

USE your Joy

The poet's measures serve anarchic joy.

—URSULA K. LE GUIN

With all of the horrible things happening in our world, we often feel guilty about being joyous. It can feel wrong to express any level of elation as our planet and fellow humans suffer. But joy is a crucial part of collective healing, and limiting happiness because of guilt only harms us as a whole. Humans don't do well with apathy. Yet I understand why so many of us feel stuck in the current climate. With genocide, institutionalized racism, police brutality, climate change, deforestation, sexism, transphobia, and inequality of all kinds plaguing the headlines, it makes sense that so many people feel powerless and are in despair.

But it's important to remember that in addition to the actions we can take by attending meetings to organize, signing petitions, voting, and voicing our outrage, our joy is a form of activism.

The poems that I wrote for my Poem Store customers had an innate optimism. I didn't set out intending to write positive poems for the masses; it's just that whatever I'm channeling when I create spontaneously for strangers is a thing of light. This hopefulness doesn't exclude the darkness or pain that a customer might present when they name their subject; rather, it's a reminder that goodness exists.

Sometimes that goodness is a lesson, the inspiring aspect of pain that causes us to grow or the stark reality of something horrific that won't last forever, that will change if we work for it or give it time. There is joy in all of this acknowledgment. There is felicity in our expressions of belief. Even a glimpse of hope in a time of hopelessness is a serum of solace that we all seek. Poetry is this medicine.

Poems can help us celebrate joyous events. To thrive amidst pain and confusion, we have to learn how to hone in on the things we're most grateful for and praise them with language.

POETRY IS A FORM OF PRAISE.

As we care for ourselves and make the most of life, as we serve and revere, as we mend our many mistakes, as we acknowledge and unpack our privilege, allowing for a release of rapturous expression feels radical and imperative.

The Pleasure of Being Alive

I wake up at dawn and find
the half moon staring in my window,
as bright as the coming sun.
What can I do but sing to honor it?
I stand on the porch and the notes
come easy, all glory for the glowing
green, grey, blue of landscape.
What else is good? Your dark eyes
that won't look away from mine.
The worn wool blanket that
keeps us warm. The pink flowers
that have yet to open in the grass.
I watch as the white light
is swallowed in fog, the apple tree
hung with glittering dew.

A Morning

I gladly keep the windows open,
desert air rushing in to cover everything
with chaparral dust. I'll wipe it up again
and again, or just let it stay. The sound
of the cat drinking. The hatchet cut
on my knuckle and the splinters in my hands.
Good to wear the mark of wood.
Old broom handles and the worn barn door.
Avocado, pine, and oak. A needle
and the slow yet satisfying meditation
of removal. I praise it all
with water for the orchard roots
and bring the hose to my lips.
I release all worry.
The earth is here and I am it.

EXERCISE for Joy

MAKE A RITUAL OF JOY

Be in service to your joy by noticing it. Let this observation be a routine, a ceremonial practice of tending to your exuberance. The more joy we feel, the better chance we have of extending such delight to others. Hallelujah! You woke up and saw the brilliant sun again! This thought is the day's first poem. Oh joy! The wilderness is large and secretive! Write about it. Wow! You are loved by a gentle woman, and she sings so sweetly. Write her a letter and find poetry to celebrate her goodness. When someone is getting married, they often write poetic vows of dedication and potent promises. When someone graduates from college, we commend them with verse. It's natural to fall into poetry when we are struck by joy. Let the work of words reveal joy in your thoughts, on the page, in any way that pays tribute to the pleasure of being alive so that you feel it fully on each occasion.

We Find Joy

And joy will be
the forever key
to our acceptance
of knowing the self fully.
So if joy leaves,
we know we have
to dig in again
to discover
the next phase
of truth.

WRITING PRACTICE

WRITE A CELEBRATORY POEM

Whether it be a momentous occasion or something simple, challenge yourself with the task of noticing your jubilation. Focus on the things you like and the happiness that they provide. Put this down on paper to remember such buoyant feelings when they are less easy to come by. Do you need to let your neighbor know how happy their sunflowers make you? Write them a short verse of thanks. Do you need to remind yourself that your job makes you happy? Write a definitive poem about why. Write about ice cream, about the TV show that makes you laugh, about the wrinkles around your father's eyes when he smiles, about the way your cat plays freely in the grass—anything that offers you joy is deserving of a few grateful lines.

Often other people are my poetry; the love they give and the delight they bring to my life are my deepest inspiration. Try writing a poetic tribute for someone you love and let your reverence flow forth freely. For me, the art of the compliment is a poetic one. If someone makes you feel wonderful, do it in return. Conjure up a gorgeous compliment and let that be the poem that stands between you.

Write a celebratory poem:

Place is also a huge source of joy. I regularly write praise poems that lift up the attributes of a landscape. Is there a place that brings you great elation? Write about it in detail to commend it and share its perfection:

To Let This Land Be My Cape

I stand before the green valley
and hear it say: *you belong,*
this is the place that fits you.

I searched for years to find
the right ravine. I traveled
the country testing canyons,
listening to the ground,
calling on rest and refuge.

Now, a hawk hangs above me
and my body is a stone
among the swaying trees.

I memorize the cakes of light
that make their way
through the canopy.
My knees are stained with mud
from spontaneous prayer
and I watch the rolling fog arrive.

I have everything I need—
it is wet and wonderfully heavy.

POETIC MINDSET TIP

FIND JOY EVERYWHERE

Most days offer a hint of something to rejoice in. Even if it's just a small cloud floating on the horizon or one kind word from a stranger on the bus, this is a drop of pleasure, and that's all that's needed for a poem to bloom in your mind. A way to ignite this type of thinking is by making lists of things that you like. My book *Go Ahead & Like It* describes this practice. Writing down lists of the particular things that I find noteworthy, the beautiful aspects of the commonplace, the little incidents that stand out in a day, changes my perspective and reminds me there are countless components that add up to create my enjoyable life. From the smallest things, like soft cotton sheets, perfectly ripe apricots, and a favorite song on the radio as I sit in traffic, to the monumental moments of celebration, they all combine to catalyze my ongoing satisfaction. My lists of likes simply reinforce and remind me of my human ability to uncover joy.

chapter 9

LISTENING TO THE POETIC UNIVERSE

The words boil out of me,
coil after coil of sinuous possibility.
The cosmos unravels from my mouth . . .

—MARGARET ATWOOD

When I'm confused, when I can't decide which way to go, when I'm looking for renewal and nothing makes sense, I turn to poetry. I fill up notebooks with rambling lines. I read the work of poets who were lost and found their way through writing. I filter my thoughts and options with logic and with unlimited compassion for the complexity of being alive. It's often hard to figure out the best move. I give myself permission to be lost sometimes, and in such moments, typically dark and hard, I can count on my connection to the universe at large to be a guiding light.

When I say "the universe," I'm talking about some kind of higher power. God, Goddess, the swirling magic of the cosmos, the Great Unknown, the Almighty Mystery, Consciousness, the force that exists behind the intricate perfection and elaborate chaos that are creation, the whole wild mess that puts atoms in their place, the sacred science of being, the miraculous human brain, the Spirit inside of it all—whatever it looks like to you, whatever you call it, it's this source that I connect with when I'm trying my best to follow some kind of lead in the dark.

As someone with immense privilege, my choices can be limitless. How do I make the best decisions for myself, for my career, and my relationships? What tools can I use to make these choices? Each day brings a new question—which step to take, which direction makes sense for me—and I've found the best way to sift through all of the questions is to create a practice around it.

Every morning and every evening I sit at an altar to get myself grounded. I light candles, burn sweet-smelling plants, sing and hum, write in my journal, ask my questions, listen to the silence around me, and look deep within my own mind. For years I've dedicated myself to this ritual; I never miss it, not even when I travel. My altar and the time I spend there every day allows me to find coherence. When I search for clarity, I'm reminded to redefine my purpose, to sharpen my reasons for being here on earth, and when I remember what it is that moves me most, there's always a poem there in one form or another.

POETRY IS AN OFFERING OF CLARITY.

How to Fall in Love with Yourself

Sit in front of two candles,
one for each eye.
Light them and watch how the fire
takes its time with the wicks, nearly dying,
touching wax and climbing back into air
with a wave of hot yes.
Now, breathe each flame into the crown
of your head. There is a hole there
where elements can enter.
Your skull is a cup, hungry for light.
Close your eyes and let
this glowing gift travel throughout
your entire body, take it down
slowly, like a dose of brilliant honey.
See how you overflow?
See how you do magic?
The warmth is red. It's white, orange,
blue and green. It touches every
part of you and when
the tailbone starts snaking,
when you become a tree,
you will love yourself completely
for burning with such ease.

EXERCISES for LISTENING TO THE UNIVERSE

HOW TO TAKE CARE SO YOU CAN HEAR IT

The surrender it takes even to ask for help is a type of poetry: saying yes to diving deeper. When we choose to care for ourselves and build a practice around this care, we open up to new possibilities of creativity. My altar is also the space I go to if I'm experiencing some kind of blockage. Some might refer to this as writer's block. If I'm ever blocked, it's not because I don't know what to write; it's more than that. It's that I haven't given myself the time or space it takes to figure out what I'm actually feeling. There's a recipe for moving through this barrier. In order to fully tune in to the universe, to clear my blockages and be open enough for the muse to enter, I have to make room and focus. Only in this pause will I be able to prepare myself for a poem that wants to arrive.

There are countless methods to make a conversation with the universe more direct and accessible. I could write an entire book on the practices that work for me, but it's really up to you to feel your way through this and build a daily ritual that's most appropriate for you and your poetic voice. Here are some of my favorite techniques for finding clarity and getting grounded.

A Room of One's Own

Do whatever you can to create a writing space for yourself: a corner of the house that's just yours or a room where you can shut the door and be with your thoughts. Solitude is such a huge part of my writing practice. In solitude, I best hear what the universe is telling me; I can hear the poems emerge. I give myself a retreat at least once a year. That means I make time for myself outside of my home, some-where special, even if it's just for one weekend, and I go there to write, to think, and to just be. I like to go to Joshua Tree for my creative seclusion. There's no temptation there to connect with other people. It's just me and the wide-open desert. Most of my greatest writing happens on retreat, when I have uninterrupted time to read through my journals, to hear my own voice, to speak each poem aloud, and to know that no one will disturb me. It can take some time to find my rhythm when I go on retreat. I'm slow to start, so I need a lot of time to settle in. Knowing this helps me plan how long I need to be away (the more time, the better), and it helps me be gentle with myself as I find my flow. And then, when it comes, it comes on fast, and nothing is in the way. Maybe you can't afford to set that much time aside and will need to craft your rhythm quickly. Maybe you'll get only a few sentences on the page. I always remind myself that it isn't the number of words that matters but the quality of time spent with my voice that's most important. Having the space to discover that is a crucial aspect of a writing practice.

A Poet Loves to Walk

So many of my favorite writers talk about the importance of walking. Thoreau wrote an entire book about it, and Mary Oliver often discusses how walking is a main part of her writing practice. In Zen Buddhism, walking can be a form of meditation. For me, the time I spend walking helps me move through thoughts I'm stuck on and ideas for writing I can't seem to push past. I always try to carry a notebook with me when I walk because I know that the motion of my steps will create newness. When the blood and the breath are moving, the mind can calm itself enough so that the voice of everything around me is that much more potent and audible. Just being outside is helpful, staring at the trees, taking off my shoes and socks to put my bare feet on the ground—but when I walk, I find a calmness in my mind like no other. While I'm walking, the world communicates with me in remarkable ways. So many of my poems and songs arrive when I'm on a walk.

The Walk to the Mailbox

When I want to send something by mail,
I make my way down the hill.
At the intersection, I slip envelopes
into the blue box and turn around
to climb back up. The Hollywood sign
is a small white phrase tucked between buildings.
I pass dogs and dirt yards, the alley
with the ficus tree, the cacti that peek
over the cement fence, bigger every year.
I step over the two squares of concrete soaked in oil
and wave to the men working on their drag racer.
There is the lot with the rooster, the driveway
with the calico cat who likes to be pet, the big
bush of rosemary where bees gather, the row
of giant Jacaranda and the fat patch of bamboo.
I breathe and move my feet. All I have to do
is a simple task. This is not a forest path,
the air is dry and the sidewalk stinks,
but I cherish it all the same.

I could also call this section "a poet needs to move" and write about all the ways in which I have to attend to my body in order to remain open and clearheaded. Writing requires a lot of sitting, and if my body hurts, I can't hear the universe as well. So I dance a lot too. I dance all the time. I stretch a lot, I get my breath going, I swim and make sure my muscles are awake and my spine has been tended to. We can't just sit there and hope for the best.

We have to get our blood flowing
for the poetry to flow as well.

Make Time for Visions and Dreams

Just as I set aside time and space for writing and walking, I make room for stillness. When I close my eyes and sink into a meditative state, I find a rush of visions swirling in my mind. If I let myself go deeper, it's typically these visions that offer a richness to my poetry. We can't just rely on our surface thoughts to make a good poem; we have to delve further into the subconscious where our unique perception dwells. This is where the good stuff comes from. The wacky, the weird, and the truly exceptional images that make a poem stand out often arrive from the depths, the inner workings of the self that go unheard and unseen if we don't give ourselves the opportunity to pay attention. For me, this means I need to sit or to lie on the floor and go inward. Sometimes when I'm at my desk writing, all I have to do is close my eyes and stare into the darkness, and a vision will drift into focus. I'll assign it to whatever idea is on the page, weaving it in as a metaphor that takes the poem to another level of potency. I also find that my visions tend to be healing for me, giving added value and explanation to difficult matters that I need to address. If we don't give ourselves time for daydreaming, we cut out a huge part of the creative process.

Try it now if you'd like. Close your eyes for a
bit and then write down whatever you see:

Equally, my dream world is a mainstay for my well-being while supplying me with a lot of insight for writing. What happens in the subconscious mind as we sleep is such a wild mystery. I get a lot of knowledge about myself from my dreams and do my best to remember them. Like most important things, it takes effort. I tend to write my dreams down in my journal or tell a friend about them. When I do this, I remember my dreams more frequently. Assigning interpretations to my dreams helps me recall them more clearly. These vivid accounts are strange and full of symbolism, great collections of useful information that churn out from the recesses of my mind as I rest. I wouldn't want to ignore or waste the opportunity to get a better look at my inner workings. Our dreams are yet another cosmic source that consistently contribute to the wealth of our self-awareness.

I often consider my dreams to be enigmatic messages, and decoding them is an illuminating, imaginative practice that buoys a lot of my poetry.

Another way I access visions happens when I'm crying. Letting yourself cry on a regular basis is an incredible source of release, and with release comes a clearing that allows for newness to enter. When I give myself the time and space to cry, to really let it all out, I usually discover a meditative place in the aftermath, and here a vision is often revealed. As an empath, I feel the entire world, and as all of that feeling builds, it can get heavy. When I'm carrying too much weight, when I'm holding a large amount of pain that isn't mine alone, I can't fully access my own pure emotions. The way I offer myself relief from the pain of the world is to cry. I realize this outpouring of tears might come more easily to some than to others, but it's important to try and break open. I'll sit or lie down and tap into my sadness in a private space where I feel comfortable enough to unfurl freely. In the aftermath of my tears, I sometimes come across a fresh interpretation of a feeling or an issue, which I'll write that down in order to remember it.

Tears

We are built to weep. Eyes
ready for release, salt set free
from our inner source, a spell
in wet song that announces
sorrow, a tender verse
that works within water
willing us toward newness.
The great strangeness of our
vessel, the function of a body
begging to let loose old weight,
deep pressure, hidden hurt.
May we bow to the overflow,
wail in wonderment, and kæt let
the cry come as a good gift,
as the rising possibility
of returning to joy.

Little Notebooks

Just as I take a notebook on my walks, I have one by my bed for when I wake up in the middle of the night with a poem. I also have one in my car so I can pull over and jot down an idea when it presents itself. I have one in my desk drawer, and I have a larger journal that I write in every day. The practice of writing down whatever comes to you whenever it decides to come is a way of showing the universe that you are here to translate it, that you are available to let this mysterious voice pulse through your mind and through your hand onto the page. I review the content of these little notebooks when I'm focused on a particular project. I flip through them when I first sit down at my desk to write and source material from the notes I left myself the day before. I find that whatever I scribble down has some significance, whether it's a simple reminder or something complicated that gets me thinking. Above all, these notebooks serve as endless inspiration. I'm never short on subject matter if I keep up with this ritual.

Treat Yourself

An important part of creativity is being kind to yourself. I find that if I'm too rigid in my practice, if I'm too hard on myself without reward, I don't write as well. If I'm gentle with myself, if I reward myself at least once a day, I feel better while I'm sitting at my desk. This reward can take whatever form you need it to: a cupcake, a glass of wine, a break to spend time with a friend, a TV show, a bath, a cup of tea, whatever works for you. Just make sure to let yourself indulge for a bit so you can better reap the benefits of diligence.

Conserve Your Energy

If you want to lean in to the voice of the universe and pull poetry from it, you have to learn how to create boundaries and conserve your energy. Each day I choose to focus on specific projects, different friends, and chosen tasks. When I'm careful about how I use my energy, I make more room for the magic of poetry to pass through me. If I extend myself too much socially, if I don't take care of my body, if I don't give myself enough time at my desk, I make it impossible to receive all the lessons that come my way when I'm tuned in to the world around me.

When I tune in with enough energy to spare, with a healthy body, and with adequate time at my desk, the muse has a good foundation to land on, and I can respond to her with my full self. By taking good care, I'm respecting the vigor required to fully show up for the craft of poetry.

One great way to conserve your energy is to collaborate. I find that when I work with friends or my publishers, when we make a project happen together and divvy up the tasks of editing, distribution, or discussing the possibilities of an idea, I'm not stretched as thin. I can rely on another person to bring their energy to the table as well. This doesn't work for everything, and poetry is all in all a very solitary art—but when I'm able to share a part of the process with someone else, I tend to feel like I have more to offer my work in general. It's true that having others involved might make things more complicated at times, but I'm also held accountable when there are other eyes on what I'm making. That feeling of accountability can actually help me avoid distraction, and I'm always looking for whatever enables me to be more available to the act of creation.

Distraction

Our many forked road,
paths so infinite
that an entire decade
can pass before we
realize we are focused
on a streetlamp
and not the moon.
Turn around, time
is a circle. Start here
where one thing is clear
and let it go wrong again
if only to finally hear
the bell ringing
its lesson. A door opens,
we remember we are
xxx limitless and suddenly
we stop looking away.

The Daily Ideal

One way I'm able to gain clarity is by checking in with my "daily ideal." This has been a favorite practice of mine for years. The first time it came up I was on retreat in the desert. I asked myself to think about what I would actually do if I had an entire day of uninterrupted time. The answer was a list, a schedule of sorts, that spelled out the most important aspects of my day. The daily ideal is basically a set of guidelines that helps me remember what a perfectly productive day looks like for me. This ideal changes with time. I adjust it to whatever state of mind I'm in, and it typically corresponds with my dedication to a certain project. Ideally, I have boundaries set up so I can efficiently get to everything I need to get to in a day to feel satisfied and fulfilled. This includes things like self-care, computer work, connecting with friends, and creative practice. Once I've refined my daily ideal to a point that feels good, I tape it on the wall in front of my desk and refer to it as I work. Sometimes the ideal is very lofty, loose, and fun. Sometimes it's quite rigid, with set times and rules. This set of directions keeps me on track and open to the work of inventiveness. It serves to guide my mind back toward the things that matter most as I let poetry move through me.

Daily Ideal

Early to rise, altar time, solitude, quiet.
Tea, journal, stretching.
Outside time, walking, breathing, being.
Work on a specific project for a decent
amount of time with a candle lit.
Internet time minimal and research based.
Eat good meals, drink a lot of water.
At least an hour a day reading a book.
Dance often, swim, run, bike, move around.
Study something new. Have fun, get wild.
Connect with one friend in a meaningful way.
Altar time again and early to bed.

Your Daily Ideal:

Use the Tools

I'm a huge fan of asking the universe for guidance, and I use all types of tools for this practice of inquiry. I have three decks of cards designed for divination, and I often choose a single card from each deck to start off my week. I'll pull a full spread of cards when I'm in need of deeper understanding. This practice is really about intuition. When I read my cards, I do use the books that come with a deck and learn from the person who created the tool, but for the most part, I delve into my own understanding of what the images and definitions mean for me. It's the initial feeling I get when I look at a card or read about it that guides me.

Strengthening your intuition is a tool that will help your poetic practice because your intuition tells you when a word is the right one to use, when an idea is worthy of your time, and when it's best to let something go that isn't working to serve your vision on the page.

You can even make your own deck or divination tool.

*Bundle up your personal wisdom and
serve it to yourself in times of need.
Your wisdom is the wisdom of the universe—
we're just star stuff, after all.*

My friend Sacha Marini suggested that we make our own "bottle cap oracles." She got the idea from her friend Sarah Brown. We collected old, flattened bottle caps for months, painted our oracle answers on them, and tossed the caps into little velvet bags that we'd pull from after asking a question. We each made our own books to pair with the bottle caps, further explaining our oracle answers. I highly suggest making your own divination tool because you'll get to see what you think you need in periods of crisis or longing. These answers show us so much about who we are. I continue to pull bottle caps from the bag when I'm lost or confused.

You can use all types of materials to make your own divination tool. Use index cards, or cut squares of paper, or paint bottle caps—whatever feels best for you. However you want it to look, come up with a collection of supportive, Magic 8-Ball answers to questions that you feel would help direct you in a time of need. Let this writing be as poetic as possible. Here are some examples to help you get started:

Bottle Cap Oracle

My personal compendium

1. How do I find balance?

Remember it's important to release yourself
from binaries and find balance instead.
Discover the possibility of synthesis
and turn toward the center.

2. Remember we know nothing.

When we get stuck on the desire for certainty,
may we recall that nobody every knows anything,
nothing is set, everything is a great mystery.

3. Timshel

Thou mayest. Remember, we always have a choice.

4. YES

A resounding positive. Infinite acceptance.

5. Onward

Sometimes it's appropriate to keep moving forward
and avoid getting weighed down in a standstill.

6. Settle In

Hold steady and settle in while finding focus.
Do not look past the current lesson.

7. Who's it for?

What are your intentions with this decision?
What is the purpose? Who or what are you serving?

Sacha showed me another method with an old dictionary, which I love. It's a fortune-telling game of sorts. You set your intention, ask a question, focus on what you're trying to see clearly, and flip open a dictionary to tell your fortune with the words on the page. Run your finger over the lines with your eyes closed and land on a word or a phrase. That landing place will be an answer you can decipher in a creative way. And you don't have to use a dictionary; any book will do. Are you confused about where to live? Open up a poetry anthology, for example, and see how something like a Wendell Berry poem about the forest makes you feel. Take direction from poetry in this way and let it show you what you want most.

A Mountain Brought Me Here

I sat in my tent as fog shifted
through the gulch. I lit my candle
and asked my questions.
Where should I be if not here?
How can I best be in service?
Where is this room of my own?
I arranged the tarot cards
in a fan for the future.
Go where you can reach everyone.
Go where you are loved already by many old friends.
Go to the place that will spread your voice the farthest.
I brushed two brown spiders
from the doorway and they curled up
like peppercorns.
Outside, I stood barefoot
in the wet grass, the sun appeared
as a full melon, a disc of light.
I stared up at Baby Tooth,
my mountain in the mist.
I asked my questions again
and this peak, so small
against the other alps, started speaking.
I heard four syllables, the name
of a hot southern city. It took me
a year to accept the invitation,
but a mountain had demanded direction
and I needed to follow its lead.

WRITING PRACTICE

WHAT ARE YOU ASKING FOR?
WHAT PATH IS ALREADY OPEN?

Use the pages here or take out your journal and write down anything that's happed today that felt like guidance, like a sign or a suggestion. Is the weather telling you to stay inside or to go outside? Do you feel rushed or ready to relax? Do you have time to write, or are you hurrying through routine tasks? How is the universe saying yes to what you truly need right now? To understand this better, first you have to know what you need!

Try writing out your own dream fortune for the day, for the week, for the year. How would you like to see your story unfold? If you could have it your way, what would it look like? Write all of these dreams down and then take note: What is the universe making easy for you? What paths have opened up? How have you tried to move in the direction of your dreams? What has gotten in your way? What lines have you already cast to help make these dreams come true?

I practice this kind of manifestation writing often, discerning what I actually want my life to look like, focusing on the potential and possibilities and then turning them into visions that I flesh out on the page. This always leads me to something succinct that I can call closer. Not something to grasp or to be too sure of, but a feeling of clarity that shows me I'm awake, listening, engaged with the signs and symbols that provide proof I'm on the right path. This path is poetic and changing. If I can remember that the universe is indeed holding me in every moment, then clarity is much more accessible. If I let the universe guide me, if I try to stay in the flow every day and note what's open to me, then I can walk forward with less resistance and vagueness. Writing about this offers me a lucid perspective that helps me consider the entire picture.

What I Want is Family

Everyone come over, get
closer, be casual, stay late
and talk about things
that matter, laugh and roll
around in ideas, silly jokes
repeated, kids barefoot,
messy, nothing perfect.
Be dramatic or quiet, eat
and cook, dance and sleep.
Do it every day or once
a week. Rely on this place
and these people, rely on
this warmth. Be familiar
with each other, shared
stories, depth or levity,
just together under our
roof, our stars, our sense
of connection relentless
and satisfying.

Future

I can't see my future clearly.
It's a wash of color and light.
Maybe a glimpse of a house
with wood floors, the death
of a parent, a dog, a cat, a love,
but nothing certain. I like its fog.
Inevitably something will happen, pieces
will fall into place if I keep breathing
and I'll eat, I'll work, I'll learn
and know and forget. There'll be
another bowl full of berries, a hot cup
of tea, additional travel and sorrow.
There'll be a clean pair of pants,
the sun's good glow, a cut and blood,
a hole to dig, a bath to take, a mistake to mend.
What lies ahead is a promise
standing in shadow, one second
pasted to the next. I don't need to call it
by name. A riddle ensues, a song of guessing,
a vow of risk. The road becomes itself
single stone after single stone
made of limitless possibility,
endless awe.

List some openings, signs, and moments of guidance that recently brought ease or clarity into your life:

What is your future vision?

POETIC MINDSET TIP

THE POWER IN MAKING POETIC MANTRAS

I'm a big fan of positive affirmations and thought patterns. I feel we can conjure up clarity by replacing our confusing thoughts with transparent, poetic ones. This is a practice of making mantras, or short poems that I can say again and again throughout the day to remain focused and unblocked. When something is hard, I like to remind myself: everything is exactly as it should be. How could it not be? This is the life we all live; it is what it is. And so, when it all seems to go astray or off-kilter it's important to remind ourselves that we are enough, doing everything we can do to show up with our best, and if we aren't showing up we can learn how to because we have all the tools we need. Poetic mantras are bits of advice we give ourselves to stay the course, keep our heads above water, and to remain clear as we let the universe show us the way. I highly recommend reading Louise Hay's book *You Can Heal Your Life* for countless affirmations that will inspire you to write your own.

I am just
an assortment
of atoms
moving through
space & time.
A great mystery
compiled in this
rare form.

chapter 10

PERMISSION TO BE A POET

And to be poetic, truly, does not mean to escape from life but does mean life raised to intense significance and higher power.

—FRANK LLOYD WRIGHT

*Y*ou have permission to love the poetic part of yourself, to work at that piece inside of you until it comes out in words, to gather up all of your swirling ideas and make sense of them in language. You can be a poet who never writes, a secret poet, a poet who appreciates the craft but keeps their journal locked away from others. You don't have to call yourself a poet to be one. This can be a private journey of naming and processing feelings. But if you're looking to give yourself over to this artistry in a more profound way, there are a few things you can commit to that will make your writing process that much more of a fine-tuned craft.

EXERCISES for BEING A POET

GIVE YOURSELF THE TOOLS

Find the Poet in Your Life

Do you know any poets personally? Maybe you're the only poet you know? Maybe your favorite poet feels like a friend because you've read their work so many times? We should all have poets in our lives, someone who alerts us to the magic within the mundane, someone who concentrates on the glorious wonder of being here on earth and condenses it into a readable contribution. Someone who asks the hard questions and answers them in fascinating and original ways; someone who must write it all down. Go out to poetry readings and find them. Let them be your mentors; let them nurture you or bring you into their circle. Ask them about their process and support their work. Hire them to edit your writing or to give advice. We all need each other, readers and writers, in a cyclical offering of appreciation and encouragement.

The Importance of Appreciation

The artist finds the holy color,
the poet searches out the sacred word,
the musician brings our silence
into song. The friend works to celebrate
each of our attempts, the elder holds us
willingly in warmth without question,
the lover remembers our wounds
and brings us the care of salve
and kiss. Might we match their efforts
with our gratitude, reminding the givers
of their worth. For what is it to live
without telling them that although
their magic can be intimidating,
it's the thing that keeps us lifted.
It's their offerings that cradle
what's hidden in our depths.

Read a Lot of Poetry

If you want to write poetry, you need to read a lot of poetry. You need to read it out loud to no one but yourself or to your best friend, your lover, your mom, your dog, your boss. Read it on the bus, in bed, in the forest, in the bathtub, in the middle of the night. You need to read it every single day. At least one poem a day. Go to your local bookstore or library and browse, flip through pages of poetry, discover your favorite poet, find the voice that you like most and devour everything by that writer. Find out which writers this writer was inspired by and joyously follow the endless lineage of language.

WHEN YOU READ A POEM,
DON'T GET HUNG UP ON
THE MEANING OF THE PIECE;
JUST ENJOY THE PARTS
THAT SPEAK TO YOU.

When I was younger, my mom told me she didn't understand poetry. I told her to let go of her notion that she needed to comprehend every word of my writing. Was there a line that jogged a memory for her? Did she see a color or smell a scent as she read this stanza? Did a word sound good to her? Did a part of the verse cause her to feel an emotion? As she answered my questions, I'd tell her, "Yes, that's it. You got it. That's what the poem is about!" She felt liberated with this direction and was finally able to take pleasure in poetry. Just choose whatever works for you in a poem and let that be enough. Once a poet publishes their work or puts it out there, it belongs to the reader, and we get to ingest it in whatever way makes sense to us.

The important thing is that we consume poetry frequently enough that it becomes a major part of how we interpret the world.

Vultures

The goat trails behind me
grabbing mouthfuls of coltsfoot
and the feathers of a vulture cut
the air above us. The sound
of such largeness in flight
is anything but gentle.

In the clearing, the sun bleeds orange
over everything, filtered by season's wildfire.
I see this bird is not alone.

Ten buzzards circling means death.
I feel no apprehension
as I try to get a glimpse of their meal
and wonder over life's secret workings.
Is there a rule for who receives today's carcass?
Who declares which belly or beak this death belongs to?

Each detail reveals some unsavory crease
that allows the whole of life to fold right.
I nod upward and the goat cocks his head
before running home full speed.

Write in a Journal

You need to write in a journal, not just on a computer. Your handwriting, the pencil on the paper, the ink on the paper—it's a spell for inspiration. My journal is the sacred center of my poetic practice. It's a sloppy, private place for tangled thoughts and ideas that I revisit often. My journal is a pep talk. It's where I build myself up, where I stand up for my inner voice, where I remind myself that I have a wild ability to fill up page after page and nothing can get in the way of that outpour. Every entry holds a key to a deeper understanding of myself, my goals, and my needs. My journal doesn't require any format, it can be a manic mess, and it's a treasure trove of material.

I leave symbols for myself in my journals so that when I sift through them, I can easily find ideas I know are meant to be bigger, ideas I want to flesh out. For example, in a long ramble about a visit to Northern California, there's an asterisk next to a section about a vulture I saw one evening when walking on the road. I wanted to remember to expand upon this scene and turn it into a poem at a later time.

← THIS IDEA
IS READY TO
COME TO FRUITION!

✳ THIS IS A
POEM

△
△ A LIST OF
△ IDEAS TO EDIT

◎ SOME KIND OF
COSMIC DRIFT TO
REVISIT

＞ LOOK AT THIS ＜

A SOLID CONCEPT
LIVES INSIDE
THIS BOX

I love going back through my journals and finding my own directions there, markings that say, *Yes, write more about this; turn back to this entry and think harder; get into it further; linger on this feeling or this occasion.* Your journal is just for you. It's your outlet, your praise, your pain and exhilaration expressed by your own hand. I can't stress enough how important it is for you to incorporate journaling into your writing ritual.

i LIKE WRITING ON A PLAIN WHITE page. i FIND IT'S EASIER TO FEEL THROUGH my IDEAS FREELY WITHOUT LINES OR BORDERS.

Try coming up with a few of your own
journaling symbols:

WRITING PRACTICE

FIND A ROUTINE AND SHOW UP FOR IT

You should write every day. It doesn't always have to be poetry, but some form of freewriting needs to happen so you can keep your muscle toned, your tool sharp, and your skill in use.

To get yourself into a freewriting ritual, try writing things down all day long: things that inspire you, scenes you notice on your drive to work, great phrases you overhear. Get into a practice and keep it steady. Witness your handwriting; fill up notebooks with rambling ideas and secret expressions. Set a timer for five minutes and write about the first object you see or the first image that comes to mind. If you start writing about something else after one sentence, that's okay—just keep going. Ramble, be free, and don't worry about making sense. This is just a way to get you to arrive with your pen and turn on your writing brain.

Develop a dedicated practice. Show up for your writing like it's a job you adore. Make it a ritual of devotion. Discipline is a huge part of the craft of poetry: you have to make time every day to sit down with your words. It doesn't have to be a long time, even ten minutes in the morning before work or a short spell before bed at night. I like to light a candle on my desk while I work on a project so I don't get distracted. I set working hours for myself and turn my phone off during that time. If I wake up in the middle of the night with an idea, I turn the light on to write it down. I get it down because the muse waits for no one. I made a vow to myself that I will not turn away from concepts or sparks of creativity even when I'm tired or busy because this is my purpose, to write.

I like to experiment with types of practice. I really enjoy paying attention to the seasons of creativity and how they link with the actual seasons. In winter I get a lot done, turn inward, and spend a lot of time alone at my desk. In spring, I typically start to share my work, giving readings and publishing books. In summer I let my writing become as social as possible, as I travel on book tours. When fall rolls around, I begin to collect myself for another winter of creation. I'm interested in this as a method of productivity and like to let the seasons influence me because it's a framework I can comprehend. It doesn't always work this way, and it's best if I'm somewhat flexible with the routine. Having an ever-developing writing practice is the only way I can complete my projects, and it's the only way I ever successfully process the things that happen to me. To fully value myself and because I am a writer, I have to show up and get the details onto the page.

What is your ideal writing practice?

How to Make a Ritual

Let it be linked to something ancient
and universal, an invitation
for old wisdom to arrive, and so begin
with fire. Burn some small leaf,
or candle wick alone, let its scent
lift up into the air as if to say: begin.
Smoke as a signal or release, ashes
coming as a reminder of all that ends
and renews again. Sing a simple song
of thanks, hold a stone, draw a symbol,
move your muscles, eat fruit, drink water,
bend low in honor, bare feet in the grass,
all of this a starting place of purpose.
All of it to hold a moment that deiearesx
declares, in pause like a prayer: here
and now the honorable energy of x focus
settles, here and now let creativity commence.

POETIC
MINDSET TIP

EVERYTHING IS A POEM;
DON'T WORRY ABOUT THE OUTCOME

You don't have to write a poem down for it to be a poem. Often as I move through my day, countless poems will pass through my body. Sometimes they're wordless, just the shivering feeling of awe that comes over me as I consider this giant universe. Sometimes I hear a full verse, and instead of trying to write it down, I simply take it as an affirmation, a voice of advice, a piece of praise in and of itself. It usually doesn't matter how often I write, but more importantly, how I feel while I'm writing. When it feels like a task, I tend to move away from my desk and let the sensation shift.

Cultivating your poetic voice might not look like letters on the page for you. It might translate into more of a mindset that you can encourage in shared conversation or that you practice in the realm of your own thoughts.

I remind myself often that being alive isn't about outcomes. My days are not made holy by tangible results, but more often, life is made significant by a blend of awareness and gratitude. If you treat everything like a poem, then everything has a chance to be important, sacred, powerful, or revolutionary, and we all have permission to enact that kind of remarkable meaning.

chapter 11

RESOURCES AND RECOMMENDED READING

Language is a city to the building of which everyone has brought a stone.

—RALPH WALDO EMERSON

*E*verything I read is typically recommended by a friend or someone I respect. I find that suggestions are the best place to start. There are so many amazing books to read, and it can be overwhelming. To figure out which book is next, I follow a loved one's advice or the guidance of an inspiring peer. Sometimes I go to a local bookstore and just let a title or a cover grab my eye. But recommended reading lists are my favorite jumping-off point when I need a new book, so I crafted my own list based on some books and poems I love.

After college, I noticed that most of my poetic heroes were white men. This was a very unsettling discovery, and since then it's been my priority to research and invest in writers with marginalized voices.

The Men in Me

Most of my muses are men.

        Old men, dead men, Zen men from the 1950s.

When I read their books I think

        these are my words.

Then I wonder if they are inside of my body, my blood.

Are they urging their language to come through my pen?

Are they whispering in my ear

asking me to bend toward their character?

        Didn't so many of them die alone, too soon?

To read more books by women, people of color, and queer writers, I look for lists and endorsements that come from folks in these communities. My library is beginning to even out and fill up with a diverse selection of inspiring voices.

My book collection is my medicine chest. Each shelf provides me with something soothing, inspiring, activating, or illuminating. Each publication is a sacred object, from the binding to the cover design. Sometimes I'll hold a book in my hand and revel in the beauty of it, waiting to read it at the right time, appreciating it as a well-crafted entity.

The following list is really just a tiny taste, a few of my first loves that lean toward the poetic or celebrate the effort of artistry. I could make an ongoing multivolume offering of recommendations at this point on my reading journey.

I'm always working on catching up to contemporary poetry, as my list feels a bit rooted in the past. I find it's reliable to delve into an exploration of the classics and discover sources of inspiration that travel through time. These words have a wide reach, and I often call on an individual verse to address a challenging emotion or to add to a celebration. My books are dog-eared and bookmarked so I can easily return to the words that heal me.

For example, the poem "In the Waiting Room" by Elizabeth Bishop changed the entire course of my life.

When visiting Florida State University (FSU) for the first time, I sat in on a poetry class where the professor read this poem aloud. I had never heard anything so arresting, so relatable, that so fully captured the phenomenon of self-realization. I decided right then and there that I'd attend FSU and study poetry. This single poem shifted my path, and I revisit it whenever I need to refresh that feeling of clear poetic direction. Similarly, the poem "He Thanks His Woodpile" by Lew Welch struck me to the core. In an instance of feeling adrift, I suddenly saw myself on the page, reflected clearly in his words. I reread this piece whenever I need a reminder that I am indeed part of some ancient family of weirdo hermit writers.

> MORE OFTEN THAN NOT,
> A POEM i LOVE GIVES ME
> A SENSE of BELONGING THAT
> i NEED TO FEEL AT EASE
> IN UNCERTAIN TIMES.

These are some poems that I revisit frequently, familiar strongholds for particular situations. Which poems have affected you? Maybe you only have a few in mind, but once you get into the practice of setting aside verses that move you, you'll end up with your own compendium of poems that you can easily return to in moments of need.

A List of Poems I Return to in Moments of Need

Poems for Conjuring Awe
"Song of Myself," Walt Whitman
"Sunflower Sutra," Allen Ginsberg
"The Fish," Elizabeth Bishop

Poems for Making Meaning
"Essay on Craft," Ocean Vuong
"What It Looks Like to Us and the Words We Use," Ada Limón

Poems for Questions and Answers
"Some Questions You Might Ask," Mary Oliver
"Singularity," Marie Howe
"Mutable Earth," Louise Glück
"Late Fragment," Raymond Carver
"A Supermarket in California," Allen Ginsberg
"Lake Echo, Dear," C. D. Wright

A Poem for the Senses
"White Flowers," Mary Oliver

Poems to Honor Simplicity
"Soil for Legs," Nanao Sakaki
"The Red Wheelbarrow," William Carlos Williams
"Keeping It Simple," Mary Ruefle

A Poem for Purpose
"Reverie in Open Air," Rita Dove

A Poem for Conjuring Visions
"From My Forehead," Alice Notley

A Poem for Time
"Hymn to Time," Ursula K. Le Guin

Poems for a Few Types of Love
"For a Stone Girl at Sanchi," Gary Snyder
"Your Hands (Stieglitz to O'Keeffe)," Mandy Kahn
"Habitation," Margaret Atwood
"What This Is Not," Mary Oliver
"An Aspect of Love, Alive in the Ice and Fire,"
    Gwendolyn Brooks

A Poem for Gratitude
"Praying," Mary Oliver

A Poem for Acceptance
"Lying in the Grass," Hermann Hesse

A Poem for Growth
"The Man Born to Farming," Wendell Berry

Poems for the Passing of Time
"The Promise," Jane Hirshfield
"History as Process," Amiri Baraka
"The Bunny Gives Us a Lesson in Eternity,"
    Mary Ruefle

A Poem for Hope

"Daybreak in Alabama," Langston Hughes

A Poem for Patience

"My Species," Jane Hirshfield

A Poem for When You Are Lost

"The Undertaking," Louise Glück

A Poem for Regret

"Meeting the Light Completely," Jane Hirshfield

Poems for Grief

"For Grief," John O'Donohue
"What the Living Do," Marie Howe
"The Wake," Rita Dove

A Poem for Despair

"Wild Geese," Mary Oliver

Poems for War

"When the War Is Over," W. S. Merwin
"Aubade with Burning City," Ocean Vuong
"Engraving: World-Tree with an Empty Beehive on
   One Branch," Jane Hirshfield

A Poem for Darkness

"You Darkness," Rainer Maria Rilke

A Poem for Fear

"A Litany for Survival," Audre Lorde

A Poem for Anger

"The Bad Old Days," Kenneth Rexroth

Poems for Death

"The Shuttles," W. S. Merwin
"The Leash," Ada Limón

Poems for Place

"I Went into the Maverick Bar," Gary Snyder
"As Good as Anything," Alice Notley
"Lying in a Hammock at William Duffy's Farm in
    Pine Island, Minnesota," James Wright

Poems That Praise Details

"The Great Black Heron," Denise Levertov
"A Step Away from Them," Frank O'Hara

Poems for Motherhood

"The Gift," Louise Glück
"That Moment," Sharon Olds
"Morning Song," Sylvia Plath
"Mothers," Nikki Giovanni

A Poem for Family

"Kin," Maya Angelou

Poems for Friendship

"Ode to My Living Friends," Sharon Olds
"An Exercise in Love," Diane di Prima

Poems for Listening to the Universe

"A Standing Ground," Wendell Berry

"Planetarium," Adrienne Rich

"How to Regain Your Soul," William Stafford

A Poem in Praise of Words

"In a Word, a World," C. D. Wright

A Poem for Discipline

"You Want a Social Life, with Friends," Kenneth Koch

A Poem for Productivity

"Apparently Wasps," Lew Welch

Poems for Poetic Permission

"How to Be a Poet," Wendell Berry

"Poetry as Insurgent Art," Lawrence Ferlinghetti

I compiled this list of singular poems to address distinct emotional states, but the entire canon by these poets is inspiring and important to me. They are some of my favorite voices, and their books continuously aid my growth as a writer. There are so many others: William Blake, CAConrad, E. E. Cummings, Meredith Clark, Franz Wright, Emily Dickinson, Jorie Graham, Philip Levine, Anne Sexton, Sappho, Leonard Cohen, Claudia Rankine, Marge Piercy, Gertrude Stein. The list goes on. Each poet gives me something different, something wholly individual and at the same time human, connective, and energizing.

I prefer to read a book of poetry cover to cover. Often the order of the poems is a narrative, or it guides the reader through a process carefully designed by the writer. So rather than reading a single poem, I like the experience of an entire volume. For example, *The Dream of a Common Language* by Adrienne Rich is perfect start to finish. I wouldn't want to decide on which section or piece to suggest by itself.

Along with whatever book of poems I'm reading, I usually read another book of fiction, nonfiction, or essays. I also love graphic novels, science fiction, and spiritual texts. These are poetic in their own right. Here's a list of a few, the ones I've read more than once, the ones that changed everything, the ones I feel are required reading. I think everyone who is trying to live a better life, discover more, feel more, and charge up their creative spirit should read these books.

Required Reading

Please Start with These

Becoming Wise, Krista Tippett
Letters to a Young Poet, Rainer Maria Rilke
The Will to Change, as well as *All About Love*, and
   anything else written by bell hooks

A Field Guide to Getting Lost, as well as *The Mother of All Questions*, and anything else written by Rebecca Solnit

Good, Wild, Sacred, Gary Snyder

Anything written by James Baldwin

Bluets, as well as *The Argonauts*, and anything else written by Maggie Nelson

Novels I Adore

East of Eden, as well as *Journal of a Novel*, and anything else written by John Steinbeck

The Heart Is a Lonely Hunter, Carson McCullers

Demian, Hermann Hesse

When Women Were Birds, Terry Tempest Williams

White Noise, Don DeLillo

The Angle of Repose, Wallace Stegner

Exit West, Mohsin Hamid

Gilead, as well as *Housekeeping*, Marilynne Robinson

Pilgrim at Tinker Creek, Annie Dillard

Anything written by Joan Didion

The Glass Castle, Jeannette Walls

Mrs. Dalloway, Virginia Woolf

Homegoing, Yaa Gyasi

Always Coming Home, Ursula K. Le Guin

A Few Others That Are Essential

Your Art Will Save Your Life, Beth Pickens

You Can Heal Your Life, Louise Hay

How Can I Help?, Ram Dass and Paul Gorman
The Body Never Lies, as well as *The Drama of the Gifted Child*, Alice Miller
Anything written by Maira Kalman
What It Is, and anything else written by Lynda Barry
What to Do When I'm Gone, Suzy Hopkins and Hallie Bateman
How to Not Always Be Working, Marlee Grace
Tiny Beautiful Things, Cheryl Strayed
Runaway, Alice Munro
The Collected Stories, Dylan Thomas
Just Kids, Patti Smith
Autobiography of Red, Anne Carson

According to Google there are nearly 130 million books published. The number of books I'll actually read in my lifetime pales in comparison. I aim to read as many as possible, to ingest the stories that come my way, the words that I'm drawn to, the authors and poets, who like magnets, pull me in. I used to go to the library and almost panic while feeling the pressure to read book after book with no end in sight. Now I celebrate the fact that there will always be something to decipher, something to learn, countless words to indulge in, one discovery and one book at a time.

AFTERWORD

People always ask me how I tap into my creativity, how I keep it coming, how I can write so quickly and with such depth on a regular basis. There's a magic to it. There's an unknown recipe moving through me, sparking my spirit ever since I was a little girl. Yet on my journey as a creative writer, as an expressive and inspired person, I've found this to be true: it takes work to be in awe, to stay uplifted, to remain engaged with the world in a poetic way. I'm always practicing, leaving time for visions, choosing to go on a walk and ponder, deciding to rise out of bed at 3:00 a.m. to write down the poem I'm dreaming up. Inspiration requires dedication. The muse demands a certain type of attention. It's glorious work, but it is indeed work. That's my best advice. Just celebrate your effort, accept that it's endless, and enjoy the process of mining the wonder out of life on earth. We have all the tools we need. Everything is a gift. Show up for it with deep devotion and it'll continue to overflow for you in limitless detail.

ACKNOWLEDGMENTS

Thank you, Marlee Grace. Without you, my dear friend, this book would still just be an idea in waiting. I love you, and I look forward to the many creations we'll make in unison.

Thank you to Kate Woodrow and Present Perfect for believing in me without a doubt and getting this book published. Thank you to Sounds True and my wonderful editor, Diana Ventimiglia, for helping me craft this project and get it into the hands of readers everywhere.

To all of my friends and loved ones who have supported and inspired my path as a poet: I appreciate you and couldn't do this work without your presence in my life.

Matt Phipps, I'm grateful as always for your editorial eye. Please write more poetry. You're really good at it.

Shelby Duncan, my Cosmic Queen, my gratitude for you is infinite as always. Thank you for your impeccable design eye and your endless, magical presence in my life.

Thank you to Sacha Marini for introducing me to so much goodness, including Sarah Brown's Bottle Cap Oracle Project and Psychic Dictionary.

The section about "finding the poet in your life" was inspired by a conversation with my dear friends Kristy Edmonds and Nora Halpern, two women who support art and poetry in constant, magical, and much needed ways.

Kathy Fletcher, I'm so grateful for our friendship and for the chance to be part of Turnaround Arts. Through this program I've been able to see firsthand the transformation that happens when I bring my poetic ideas into the classroom.

To the Florida State University English Department, thank you for the various lessons that still enrich my writing.

Above all, thank you to the poets, living and dead, published or not, for delving into the depths and translating the darkness for us all.

Poem Sources

"In Awe" first appeared in *The Edge of the Continent Volume Two: The City* (Rare Bird Books, 2019)

"Drinking Water" first appeared in *The Edge of the Continent Volume One: The Forest* (Rare Bird Books, 2018)

"Housemates" first appeared in *The Edge of the Continent Volume Two: The City* (Rare Bird Books, 2019)

"Heart Rock" first appeared in *Help in the Dark Season: Poems* (Write Bloody Publishing, 2019)

"I'm Here" first appeared in *The Edge of the Continent Volume Two: The City* (Rare Bird Books, 2019)

"The Great Command" first appeared in *The Edge of the Continent Volume Three: The Desert* (Rare Bird Books, 2020)

"I Can Stay" first appeared in *The Edge of the Continent Volume Two: The City* (Rare Bird Books, 2019)

"Alongside Highway 299" first appeared in *The Edge of the Continent Volume One: The Forest* (Rare Bird Books, 2018)

"Without You" first appeared in *The Edge of the Continent Volume Three: The Desert* (Rare Bird Books, 2020)

"It Is Hard to Be Alive" first appeared as a greeting card for Red Cap Cards (February 2019)

"The Relief of Our Endless Becoming" first appeared as the "Weekly Quote" in Belletrist's June 2019 newsletter (belletrist.com)

"Knuckle Tattoo" first appeared in *The Edge of the Continent Volume One: The Forest* (Rare Bird Books, 2018)

"Heart Song II" first appeared in *Help in the Dark Season: Poems* (Write Bloody Publishing, 2019)

"No Siblings" first appeared in *Help in the Dark Season: Poems* (Write Bloody Publishing, 2019)

"How I Fell in Love with the Earth" first appeared in *Help in the Dark Season: Poems* (Write Bloody Publishing, 2019)

"A Morning" first appeared in *The Edge of the Continent Volume Three: The Desert* (Rare Bird Books, 2020)

"To Let This Land Be My Cape" first appeared in *The Edge of the Continent Volume One: The Forest* (Rare Bird Books, 2019)

"How to Fall in Love with Yourself" first appeared in *Help in the Dark Season: Poems* (Write Bloody Publishing, 2019)

"The Walk to the Mailbox" first appeared in *The Edge of the Continent Volume Two: The City* (Rare Bird Books, 2019)

"A Mountain Brought Me Here" first appeared in *The Edge of the Continent Volume Two: The City* (Rare Bird Books, 2019)

"Future" first appeared in *Help in the Dark Season: Poems* (Write Bloody Publishing, 2019)

"Vultures" first appeared in *The Edge of the Continent Volume One: The Forest* (Rare Bird Books, 2018)

"The Men in Me" first appeared in *The Edge of the Continent Volume One: The Forest* (Rare Bird Books, 2018)

All other typewritten poems were created by Jacqueline Suskin spontaneously in three minutes or less.

About
The Author

Jacqueline Suskin is a poet based in Northern California. She is the author of *The Collected* (Publication Studio, 2010), *Go Ahead & Like It* (Ten Speed Press, 2014), *The Edge of The Continent Volume One: The Forest* (Rare Bird Books, 2018), *The Edge of the Continent Volume Two: The City* (Rare Bird Books, 2019), *Help in the Dark Season: Poems* (Write Bloody Publishing, 2019), and *The Edge of the Continent Volume Three: The Desert* (Rare Bird Books, 2020). Known for her project Poem Store, Suskin composes improvisational poetry for patrons who choose a topic in exchange for a unique verse. From 2009–2019, Poem Store was her main occupation, taking her around the world writing more than forty thousand spontaneous poems. Her work has been featured in the *New York Times*, *T* magazine, the *Los Angeles Times*, *The Atlantic*, and other publications.

ABOUT SOUNDS TRUE

Sounds True is a multimedia publisher whose mission is to inspire and support personal transformation and spiritual awakening. Founded in 1985 and located in Boulder, Colorado, we work with many of the leading spiritual teachers, thinkers, healers, and visionary artists of our time. We strive with every title to preserve the essential "living wisdom" of the author or artist. It is our goal to create products that not only provide information to a reader or listener but also embody the quality of a wisdom transmission.

For those seeking genuine transformation, Sounds True is your trusted partner. At SoundsTrue.com you will find a wealth of free resources to support your journey, including exclusive weekly audio interviews, free downloads, interactive learning tools, and other special savings on all our titles.

To learn more, please visit SoundsTrue.com /freegifts, or call us toll-free at 800.333.9185.

sounds true
WAKING UP THE WORLD